Washington Farmers' Markets

Cookbook & Guide

Kris Wetherbee

— A Maverick Publication —

ISBN 0-89288-278-6

Library of Congress Catalog Card Number: 99-74676

Photographs on pages 8, 15, 32, 35, 51, 61, 63, 113,
and 162 courtesy of Rick Wetherbee

Maverick Publications, Inc.
P.O. Box 5007
Bend, Oregon 97708

Table of Contents

To my mom and dad
who always taught me that I could do anything,
and to my mother-in-law, Jean, who gave me
the best thing that ever happened to me,
my husband Rick.

Acknowledgments

Thank you to all the farmers' market vendors and market directors who contributed their time to share their markets and recipes for this book. Having been on both sides, I am intensely aware and grateful for the fabulous produce and products they bring to your communities. Without their delicious fresh food products, healthy plants, and beautiful hand-crafted goods, life would indeed lose flavor.

To those of you who buy this book—thank you—and I hope it encourages you to shop at your local farmers market, try new foods, and brings you good health. For saying "let's do it again", I would like to thank Gary Asher. And my biggest thanks to my husband Rick for his endless hours of assistance, patience, understanding, and loving me more than I ever thought possible.

Introduction

Farmers' markets have always been an important part of people's lives, both for shoppers and producers. An integral part of history, farmers' markets have also been an important element throughout the community by keeping farmlands in production, supplying jobs, establishing community interaction, helping the local economy and also providing the community with locally grown and just picked produce in a fun and enjoyable atmosphere.

Before the 1950's, farmers' markets were often known as public markets and were quite popular. Actually they have been a universal element of everyday life since the beginning of time. In the early 1900's, public markets were located in more than 50% of those American cities with populations of 30,000 or more. And they kept their standing as the leading market center until the upheaval of World War II.

The way Americans shopped for food also changed with the transformation of modern day transportation methods and refrigeration. First it was the railroads, then after 1955 it was the interstate highway system and mass trucking. Refrigeration extended the life of food, and corporate controlled supermarkets and processing plants soon dotted the land and dominated the food industry.

The clothing style of the 70's will always be unforgettable, and so will the "back to the land" movement that swept the country with a growing concern for pesticide-free produce that was fresh and flavorful. A reawakening began and within the last 20 years farmers' markets have spread like wildfire. Every year new markets continue to spring forth and today there are nearly 2,700 farmers' markets nationwide with over 50 markets in Washington.

Washington Farmers' Markets provide a wealth of experience and family-tested recipes from a diversity of growers and producers. Out of necessity and years of practice they have discovered ways to cook with the seasons that the whole family enjoys and so can you.

This book will provide the smart shopper with many unique and wonderful recipes, some quite challenging, and most incredibly easy. But they're all an adventure into a colorful and appetizing world of foods alive with flavors you may never have experienced before. Selection is boundless with heirlooms and other specialty varieties that can't be found in supermarkets because of their rigorous handling and transportation time involved with packing sheds and wholesalers. Freshness, flavor and nutrition are much higher with prices often being generally lower (especially during the peak harvest season) than for most comparable items found in the supermarkets. And many health-conscience farmers are growing their foods without the use of pesticides and other harmful chemicals. Growing this way is not only good for the land, it's great healthy food for you and your family.

Today, most farmers' markets don't just begin or end with produce. You'll discover a bounty of specialty food items like cheese, herbal vinegars, jams and jellies, eggs that make others pale in comparison (literally), baked goods, meats and fresh-caught fish. Fresh flowers and hand-crafted goods bring a refreshing style to gift giving and our own enjoyment. And, for you gardeners or those wanting to try, the enormous selection of varieties in bedding plants, food plants, herbs, flowers, perennials, and landscape plants are every gardeners' paradise.

Bring the whole family and enjoy the best of the earth—a new experience that includes vine and tree-ripened foods, a wide selection of plants, local crafts and lots of activities. Farmers' Markets are the place to shop and a great place to be.

Shopping the Market

Trips to the farmers' market have become an anticipated event all over the country. For many, it's a weekly get together with good friends and great food. As a market vendor myself for seven years, my husband and I look forward to seeing familiar faces and hearing the latest news from our customers. I've also learned some valuable tips along the way to help make the shopping day productive and fun.

First, get to know your vendors. Walk through the market to see what each vendor has to offer. Things can change weekly, so make the rounds each time. You'll soon discover what is available and when it's available. By asking questions, you'll also learn where you can place special orders or buy in bulk. They can tell you how their products are grown, how to prepare and store foods they sell, and identify different varieties. They're always willing to share their experience with you, whether it's how to grow a plant or how to cook a vegetable.

Shop with the seasons and be flexible on menu choices. You're not likely to find fresh blackberries in June for that pie, but cherries are in season and make an outstanding pie, that is if there are any left! Sugar snap peas and asparagus may not be on your list but they may be at the market, for a limited time only. You may also see something you've never tried before. Experiment, explore and venture into a new taste experience which may become a family favorite.

For the best selection of produce at its prime, shop early. Growers may have a limited supply on the items you're looking for, particularly when it's the first of the season, and they may sell out early. Once you do see what you want don't wait too long to buy it, especially if there are only a few left. By the time you've finished looking, the item may already be sold out by the time you get back. You can often leave purchases with the vendor when space allows until you're done shopping.

Bring your own bags or baskets, and a ready cooler in the car comes in handy on hot days or when you're purchasing perishables like cheese or fish. After all, you bought them fresh and you want to keep them fresh.

To make your farmers' market experience complete, use this book. It was created with you in mind. There's a list for all the farmers' markets in Washington so you can be sure to find the one nearest you. Information is given on participating markets and vendors to bring awareness to special events, specialty items and produce available. Helpful advice on growing and cooking along with interesting history and facts are located throughout the book. And best of all are the "fresh from the farm" recipes that will make not only shopping for produce more fun, but also bring new life and excitement to your family meals. See you at the market!

Rhubarb Jam · Zucchini Jam

Hot 'N Honey Dip · France Dijon Mustard

Shrimp Dressing · Cucumber Relish

Little Brother Steve's Beef Jerky

Chinese Cabbage Salad

Navy Bean Soup · Glazed Onions

Dilly Beans · German Cabbage Balls

Baked Meatballs · Pizza Casserole for a Crowd

Best Wild Duck I Ever Tasted · Oriental Beef Pot Roast

Gramm's Granola · Heavenly Zucchini Bread

Rhubarb Muffins · No Bake Cookies

Rhubarb Swirl

Strawberry Glace Pie · Cooked Apple Cake

BELFAIR FARMERS' MARKET

LOCATION:
Highway 3 across from Theler Center
at the Belfair Elementary School
May thru October
Saturdays, 9:00 a.m. - 3:00 p.m.

FOR A FRIENDLY AND FAMILY ATMOSPHERE WITH A REAL SENSE OF COMMUNITY, the Belfair Farmers' Market is the perfect gathering place to meet up with friends and neighbors. First started in 1992 under the sponsorship of the North Mason Chamber of Commerce, the Market is now going strong into their 7th year.

This quaint Market features seasonal fresh fruits and vegetables, all locally grown by farmers and gardeners in the area. There's no better place to find fresh cut flowers to brighten your home or to share with your friends and family. Treat yourself to the delicious flavor of home baked goods by the area's best bakers. And if your stumped for that perfect gift, check out the beautiful hand-crafted goods including hand-sewn needle crafts.

You may even happen upon that special occasion to enjoy live music, taste delicious samples from cooking demonstrations, or swing your partner with some lively square dancing put on by the folks who love to share their talents with those who come to enjoy this friendly community atmosphere.

Rhubarb Jam

What started out as a hobby soon bubbled in a successful soapmaking business for Mandy and Bev Wendell, owners of Tahuya Soap Opera Herbal Soaps. The Wendell's sell quite an array of soaps at the Belfair Farmers' Market. Soaps are made all natural; no tallow, no suet, all vegetable herbal soaps with tempting ingredients like olive oils, coconut oils, palm kernel oils, shea butter, apricot kernel oil, almond oils, and macadamia nut oils.

In a jam? Try rhubarb, the perfect Northwest food for a quick and easy spread.

5 to 6 cups diced rhubarb
4 1/2 cups sugar
1 can cherry pie filling (liquefied in blender)
3 ounce package of Strawberry Jello

MICROWAVE RHUBARB until tender. Combine in a large saucepan, cooked rhubarb and sugar. Cook rapidly for 5 minutes, stirring constantly. Add pie filling and cook for 6 minutes more. Remove from heat and add Jello. Stir until dissolved. Refrigerate, or put into freezer-safe plastic containers or jars, and freeze. Makes 3 1/2 pints.

Bev & Mandy Wendell
TAHUYA SOAP OPERA

Zucchini Jam

Beatrice Riedel brings her crocheted items to the Belfair Farmers' Market, including her specialty 3-piece towel sets.

Whenever that zucchini glut comes on, this jam is one nice way to use zucchini.

6 cups peeled and grated zucchini
1/2 cup fresh lemon juice
6 cups sugar

8 ounce can crushed pineapple
6 ounce package Orange-flavored Jello

COOK ZUCCHINI in lemon juice in a saucepan until almost dry and transparent, about 6 minutes. Add sugar and crushed pineapple. Boil for 6 minutes more, stirring frequently. Add Jello and stir until well dissolved. Refrigerate or freeze.

Beatrice Riedel

Hot 'n Honey Dip

Sandra J. Randall's love for bees soon evolved into Terry's Honey. Randall sells flavored honeys like fire-weed, raspberry, and wildflower, plus wax items and candles at the Belfair Farmers' Market. And since bee education is important to Sandra, she regularly brings an observation hive to the market. She is also quite active in teaching about bees to the public schools.

The following two sauces (Hot 'N Honey Dip and France Dijon Mustard) are great for a number of dishes. Try either as a dip for vegetables, French fries, or as a sauce for meat or any hot vegetable dish.

1 1/2 cups honey
1 1/2 cups Dijon-style mustard
1 tablespoon Worcestershire sauce

1/2 teaspoon black pepper
Pinch of cayenne pepper

BEAT ALL INGREDIENTS together and serve as dip or as sauce.

Sandra J. Randall
TERRY'S HONEY

France Dijon Mustard

Spicy zip with a subtle wine flavor.

2 cups dry white wine
1 large onion, chopped (about 1 cup)
2 cloves garlic, minced
4 ounce can dry mustard

2 tablespoons honey
1 tablespoon canola oil
2 teaspoons salt
Several drops bottled red pepper sauce
   to taste

COMBINE WINE, onion and garlic in a small saucepan; boil, lower heat and simmer about 5 minutes. Pour wine mixture into a bowl; allow to cool. In a small sauce pan, add dry mustard and strained wine mixture, stir constantly until sauce is very smooth. Blend together, honey, oil, salt and red pepper sauce into the mustard mixture. Heat slowly, stirring constantly until mix thickens. Allow to cool. Pour into a non-metallic container; cover, chill in refrigerator at least two days. Makes about 2 cups.

Sandra J. Randall
TERRY'S HONEY

Shrimp Dressing

JoAnn and Robert Herrick sell regularly at the Belfair Farmers' Market, where they bring expert crafts-manship in quality furniture made out of oak and cedar.

This 'dressing' is wonderful combined with a tossed green salad.

1 cup sour cream
1/4 teaspoon salt
1/4 cup chili sauce
2 tablespoons drained pickle relish

1 tablespoon minced green onion
1 teaspoon lemon juice
1/2 pound salad-sized shrimp

COMBINE ALL INGREDIENTS together in a medium bowl. Chill and serve. About 30 calories per tablespoon.

JoAnn Herrick

companion planting chart

Here are some favorite plant combinations used by gardeners throughout the years. Test them out in your own garden and see how they work for you.

PLANT	HIGHEST BENEFITS TO	EFFECT	COMMENTS
Basil	asparagus, peppers, lettuce, tomatoes	1, 3	enhances growth, repels flying insects
Beans	potatoes, beets, squash, lettuce, cucumbers, carrots, corn	1, 4	deters potato beetles
Borage	squash, tomatoes, strawberries	1, 3, 4	provides minerals and repels tomato worm
Calendula	broccoli, cabbage, corn, beans, peas, spinach	2	attracts minute pirate bugs and lacewings
Chamomile	all garden plants	1, 2, 3	improves crop yields, attracts parasitic wasps, lady bugs, lacewings
Chives	tomatoes, carrots, apples, berries, grapes, roses	1, 3	deters Japanese beetles, aphids
Dill	cabbage family, cucumbers, lettuce, onions	2, 3	improves growth/flavor of cabbage family
Garlic	tomatoes, cane fruits, fruit trees	1, 3	repels potato blight, also use as spray
Geraniums	cabbage family, grapes, roses	1	repels cabbage worms, Japanese beetles (use white varieties)
Goldenrod	all garden plants	1, 2	attracts big-eyed bugs, ground & soldier beetles
Marigolds	all garden plants	1, 2, 3	repels aphids, potato and squash bugs; long-term use kills nematodes
Nasturtiums	all garden plants	1, 3	deters many pest bugs, attracts black fly
Onions	most crops, except peas or beans	1	deters many pests, especially maggots
Petunias	eggplant, grapes, greens	1	also plant with any vegetable bothered by leaf hoppers
Potatoes	bean, cabbage family, corn, melons	1, 2	repels bean beetles
Radishes	beans, carrots, cucumbers, lettuce	1	repels cucumber beetles
Sage	cabbage family, carrots, tomatoes	1, 2, 3	deters cabbage moths, carrot flies
Summer Savory	beans, peas, onions	2, 3	generally beneficial
Tomatoes	asparagus, carrots, cabbage	1, 3	tomatoes and asparagus are mutually beneficial
Yarrow	most aromatic herbs	2, 3	attracts parasitic wasps, lady bugs, tachinid flies

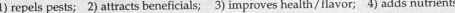

1) repels pests; 2) attracts beneficials; 3) improves health/flavor; 4) adds nutrients

Cucumber Relish

A family-owned farm since 1950, three generations now work to make Davis Farm what it is today. Famous for their green beans, beets, and pickling cucumbers, Davis Farm also brings a host of delicious produce to the Belfair, Gig Harbor, and Kitsap Farmers' Markets like squash, corn, potatoes, strawberries and raspberries. Grass and oat hay, cut flowers, perennial plants and eggs complete the list.

This recipe can be used for zucchini relish. Just substitute zucchini for cucumbers.

4 quarts coarsely ground cucumbers
2 quarts chopped onions
1 green pepper, chopped
1 red pepper, chopped
5 tablespoons salt
6 cups sugar

6 cups vinegar
2 tablespoons turmeric
1 1/2 teaspoons celery seed
1 tablespoon mustard seed
1/4 teaspoon ground cloves

ADD SALT TO cucumbers, onions, and peppers; let stand for two hours; drain well. Place vegetables in large kettle; add rest of ingredients. Bring to a boil; simmer 4 minutes.

Pack into clean hot pint-sized jars and seal. Process in a boiling-water canner for 5 minutes. Makes approximately 8-10 pint jars.

Davis Family Farm

Little Brother Steve's Beef Jerky

High-protein and delicious. Have plenty on hand.

2 to 2 1/2 pounds round or flank steak
1/4 cup soy sauce
1/4 cup red wine
2 tablespoons Worcestershire sauce
1 tablespoon hickory smoke salt
1 tablespoon honey

1 teaspoon coarse black pepper
1/2 teaspoon onion powder
1/2 teaspoon garlic powder
1 bay leaf, finely chopped
1/4 teaspoon ginger

POUR ALL INGREDIENTS (except meat) into a stainless steel or Pyrex sauce pan (never aluminum); stir and slowly bring to a boil. Cool, then skim most of the chopped bay leaves from surface. This is now your marinade for the beef.

Prepare meat; trim well and cut into strips, about 1/8 to 1/4-inch thick. Pour 1/2 cup of marinade into large baking dish. Pack strips in one layer. Pour remaining marinade into dish. Allow to stand at least 2 hours at room temperature. Turn strips every so often.

In a preheated 150 degree oven, place strips evenly spaced on rack; dry at least 6 hours. Occasionally blot strips with a paper towel. Turn strips after 3 hours. Remove from oven, blot with paper towel and cool.

Sandra J. Randall
TERRY'S HONEY

Chinese Cabbage Salad

Makes a delicious large salad that will bring rave reviews at any pot-luck.

TOSS THE FOLLOWING ingredients in a large bowl:

1 medium head cabbage, chopped
1 bunch green onions, chopped
1 cup sliced fresh mushrooms

2 small cans water chestnuts
1 cup chopped celery
10 ounce can cashews, halved

MIX WELL the following ingredients, then pour dressing over salad and toss together.

1 cup mayonnaise
2 tablespoons soy sauce
1 teaspoon sugar

When ready to serve, add one large can of Chinese noodles. Makes one pot-luck size salad.

Bev & Mandy Wendell
TAHUYA SOAP OPERA

Glazed Onions

A great side dish that's incredibly different and delicious.

4 tablespoons butter, melted
3 tablespoons lemon juice

6 tablespoons honey
3 1/2 cups onions

SAUTÉ ONIONS IN BUTTER until translucent. Add lemon juice and honey; stir and cook over low heat about 8 minutes or until onions are well glazed. Serves 6 to 8.

Sandra J. Randall
TERRY'S HONEY

pickles with a snap	Crisp pickles begin with fresh pickling cucumbers. They should be firm and show no signs of shriveling or yellowing. Ask the grower when the cucumbers were picked, quality pickles will come from cucumbers that were picked within a few days of use. Pickling cucumbers can be any size, up to 6 inches long. The larger picklers are great for making into bread and butter or dill pickle slices, the smaller ones are good for sweet gherkin pickles. For an extra crisp pickle, try adding one or two grape leaves into each jar. Seedless cucumbers (sometimes called burpless) also result in a crunchier pickle.

Navy Bean Soup

Almost 50 years ago when times were hard, we frequently had bean soup for dinner with corn bread. Dad used to coax us to eat by allowing us to add sugar to the soup. We grew up liking it this way, only now I use honey in place of the sugar.

2 cups navy beans
3 quarts water
1 tablespoon minced onion
1/2 teaspoon celery salt
2 teaspoons salt

1/8 teaspoon pepper
1/4 teaspoon mustard
4 tablespoons flour
1 tablespoon minced parsley
Honey to taste

SOAK BEANS OVERNIGHT in a large pot in enough water to cover; drain. Add 3 quarts water, onion and celery salt; cook until beans are very soft, about 1 to 2 hours. Press beans through a coarse sieve, (mom mashed with a potato masher); return to pot. Add salt, pepper and mustard. Melt butter in a saucepan, blend in flour to form a thick paste. Add paste to bean soup. Heat to boiling, stirring constantly, and cook for 5 minutes. Serve garnished with parsley and honey. Serves 8 to 10.

Sandra J. Randall
TERRY'S HONEY

Dilly Beans

Norma Stencil and Donna Beuhler joined together to form Me & Mom, and have been market vendors since the start of the Belfair Market. There specialty is their homemade pies and sticky buns. Me & Mom also offers an assortment of home-baked goods, pickled goods, and Native American crafts.

For a tasty variation, try substituting fresh corn or asparagus for the green beans.

3 pounds green beans
3 cups water

3 cups white vinegar
1/3 cup salt

BRING TO BOIL the water, vinegar, and salt to make a brine. Pack whole green beans into hot wide-mouth quart-sized jars. To each quart add the following:

1 teaspoon mustard seed
1 teaspoon dill seed

2 cloves garlic
2 teaspoons crushed red pepper *

*Or substitute fresh Jalapeno or any hot pepper of choice.

Pour hot brine into jars, leaving a 1-inch head space. Place lids and process in boiling-water canner for 20 minutes. Makes approximately 4 quarts.

Norma Stencil & Donna Beuhler
ME & MOM

German Cabbage Balls

Cabbage balls are the perfect all-around food; great served as an appetizer, a side dish, or even for the main course.

1 large head of cabbage
2 pounds ground beef
2 eggs
1 teaspoon honey (more to taste)
2 slices bread, crumbled
1 medium onion

bacon drippings
1/4 to 1/2 cup beef broth
2 teaspoons caraway seed,
   powdered if desired

BOIL CABBAGE until leaves easily separate; set aside to cool. In a large bowl, mix together ground beef, eggs, honey, onion, bread crumbs, salt and pepper. Carefully separate individual cabbage leaves from head. Fill cabbage leaves with ground beef mix and roll into balls. Melt bacon drippings in a skillet and brown the cabbage balls evenly on all sides. Add 1/4 to 1/2 cup of beef broth. Add caraway and simmer for 20 to 30 minutes. Makes approximately 32 cabbage balls.

Sandra J. Randall
TERRY'S HONEY

Baked Meatballs

This is a 'can do' ahead of time recipe that's very easy to make. Use in spaghetti sauce, sweet and sour sauce, or add to gravy. Can also freeze ahead of time.

2 pounds ground beef
1 large egg
1/2 cup plain bread crumbs
2 tablespoons dried minced onion

2 tablespoons parsley
1 tablespoon garlic salt
1/2 teaspoon pepper

HEAT OVEN TO 400 degrees. Line a cookie sheet with aluminum foil. In a large bowl, mix all ingredients together; form into balls using a heaping tablespoon for each ball. Bake 15 minutes until browned and no longer pink in the middle. Makes 32 balls.

JoAnn Herrick

Pizza Casserole For A Crowd

Tina Fugman sells homemade jams and jellies, plus quilted and crocheted items at the Belfair Farmers' Market. She has been with the market since its beginning.

We use this recipe at our church's weekly out-reach meal. It's one of our family favorites.

4 pounds spaghetti noodles, broken into 2 to 3-inch pieces
5 to 7 quarts prepared spaghetti sauce
3 to 4 pounds sliced pepperoni
Optional toppings: olives, mushrooms, onions, peppers
1 1/2 pounds shredded Monterey Jack cheese
1 1/2 pounds shredded Mozzarella cheese

COOK SPAGHETTI NOODLES according to package directions; drain. In six greased 13 x 9 x 2-inch baking pans, spread a layer of noodles. Add a layer of sauce over the noodles, then top with pepperoni and any of the other 'options'. Bake, uncovered, in a 350 degree oven for 30 minutes. Sprinkle cheese and distribute evenly over each pan. Bake 15 minutes longer or until tops are golden and bubbly. Makes about 50 servings.

Tina Fugman

Best Wild Duck I Ever Tasted

Deborah and Jack Pigott of Penible Farms helped to start the Belfair Farmers' Market. They now grow a variety of vegetables, raise chickens, tend their tree farm, and Jack makes wooden toys and trellises for the home and garden.

This duck recipe was given to us by a couple of old duck hunters.

2 or 3 skinned wild ducks	1/4 teaspoon basil
1 cube butter or margarine	1/4 teaspoon oregano
1 cup flour	salt and pepper to taste
1 medium onion, thinly sliced	1 bottle Almaden wine
1/4 teaspoon rosemary	

FIRST CUT DUCK into even-size pieces. Flour pieces and brown in a cast-iron skillet with butter. As pieces brown, move to a single layer in a deep pot; save drippings.

To the first layer of duck in pot, add onion, then layer with remaining duck. Pour in drippings from skillet; add seasonings, 1cup wine, and 1 cup water. Bring to boil; cover and turn down to simmer for 15 minutes. Turn all pieces over in pot. (Taste wine to see if it's still fresh in bottle!) Then pour more wine over duck until the level is well in sight. Cover pot and cook for 30 minutes more; checking to turn pieces if needed. (Taste wine again.)

Add a dash more wine to the duck; cover and finish cooking for about 20 to 30 minutes more. Duck should be tender by now and almost fall off the bone. Serve with mashed potatoes, as the gravy in your pot is great by now. I suggest French bread and string beans on the side, and maybe a glass of wine, that is if there is any left!! Serves 4.

Jack & Deborah Pigott
PENIBLE FARMS

---

honey hints

- Store honey at room temperature, never refrigerate. Keep tightly covered and in a dry place.
- If honey becomes crystallized, place the container in hot water until the honey liquifies and becomes clear.
- When measuring honey, first coat the measuring utensil with a small amount of oil to prevent the honey from sticking.
- Never add water to honey in the container, this may cause it to spoil. Honey will never go bad if handled and stored properly.
- When baking with honey, lower temperature 25 degrees to prevent over browning.

honey ideas

Honey is more than just a breakfast item. Many dishes that call for sugar can be substituted with honey instead. Honey can often intensify the flavor of other spices, so begin with small amounts at first. And honey is also a wonderful way to bake in flavor and keep baked goods deliciously moist. Here are a few tasty combinations for you to try.

- Honey glaze on baked squash
- Honey candied yams or carrots
- Drizzle honey over ice cream
- Drizzle honey over hot cereal
- Add honey to your favorite bread recipe
- Drizzle on cantaloupe and other fruits

Oriental Beef Pot Roast

A family favorite with lasting flavor.

1 teaspoon garlic salt
1/2 teaspoon dry mustard
1/4 teaspoon pepper
4 pound pot roast
2 tablespoons oil
1 cup water

1/4 cup soy sauce
1 tablespoon honey
1 tablespoon vinegar
1 1/2 teaspoons celery seed
1 teaspoon ginger
2 tablespoons cornstarch

COMBINE GARLIC SALT, mustard and pepper together in small bowl; rub evenly all over roast. In a large kettle, brown roast on all sides in oil. Combine 3/4 cup water, soy sauce, honey, vinegar, celery seed and ginger; pour over meat. Simmer covered for 2 hours or until tender. Remove meat to large platter; skim fat from drippings. Blend cornstarch into 1/4 cup water. Stir into drippings; cook until thickened. Serve as gravy on the side.

Sandra J. Randall
TERRY'S HONEY

Gramm's Granola

A healthy snack anytime, anywhere.

3 1/2 cups regular rolled oats
1 cup shredded coconut
3/4 cup wheat germ
3/4 cup sliced almonds*
2/3 cup brown sugar (optional)

1/2 cup powdered milk
1/3 cup honey
1/4 cup vegetable oil
dried fruits (optional)

*Or mix your favorites; sunflower seeds, chopped pecans, filberts, etc.

PREHEAT OVEN to 325 degrees. Grease a 16 x 11 x 2-inch baking dish with shortening; set aside. In a large bowl, combine oats, coconut, wheat germ, almonds, powdered milk, and any other options you choose; mix well. In small saucepan, blend honey and oil, heat gently to dissolve the honey. Pour honey mixture into dry ingredients and stir well to thoroughly coat. Spread granola evenly into the baking pan. Bake 15 to 20 minutes until evenly toasted; stirring every 5 minutes. Cool well and store at room temperature in an airtight container. Makes about 9 1/2 cups.

Sandra J. Randall
TERRY'S HONEY

makes 2 loaves
350° 50 min

Heavenly Zucchini Bread

Della Robinson's specialty is dahlias, but she also brings plenty of bedding plants, cut flowers, birdhouses, and planters to the Belfair Farmers' Market.

The flavor combination of zucchini with bananas is absolutely heavenly.

3 eggs
3/4 cup oil
2 small bananas
2 cups sugar
1 teaspoon vanilla
3 cups flour
1 teaspoon salt

1 teaspoon baking powder
2 teaspoons baking soda
3 teaspoons cinnamon
2 tablespoon cocoa
2 cups grated zucchini
1 cup chopped dates
1 cup chopped nuts

BEAT TOGETHER eggs, oil, bananas, sugar, and vanilla in a large bowl. In a separate bowl, combine flour, salt, baking powder, baking soda, cinnamon, and cocoa; stir well. Add dry ingredients to egg/oil mixture and gently mix. Stir in zucchini, chopped dates and walnuts. Grease and flour two 9-inch loaf pans and pour in batter. Bake in a preheated 350 degree oven for 50 minutes. Makes two loaves.

Della Robinson
ROBINSON'S

No Bake Cookies

Devaneys Crafts is more than just woodcrafts, Ron and Cookie Devaney also sell lots of oyster clams when they're in season.

Walnuts and filberts are in abundance at many farmers' markets. Either taste delicious in these cookies.

24 graham crackers, crushed fine
1 cup chopped dates
1 cup chopped walnuts or filberts
2 1/2 cups small marshmallows

1/4 teaspoon vanilla
1 can sweetened condensed milk
Shredded coconut

MIX TOGETHER ALL ingredients in a large bowl. Form into small balls, about a heaping tablespoon for each ball. (Chilling the ingredients first may make it easier to handle.) Roll each ball in coconut. Makes 30 cookies.

Ron & Cookie Devaney
DEVANEYS CRAFTS

Rhubarb Muffins

Over at Tall Firs Garden, Norma and Ludwig Peters are busy working on a diversity of wood and sewing crafts, including patio chairs, quilt racks, and wishing wells. And any time that's left is devoted to their flower and vegetable plants, all of which they bring to the Belfair Farmers' Market.

After making these muffins, rhubarb may just become one of your favorite vegetables.

1 1/4 cups brown sugar
1/2 cup oil
1 egg, slightly beaten
2 teaspoons vanilla
1/4 teaspoon black walnut flavoring
1 cup buttermilk

1 1/2 cups diced rhubarb
1/2 cup chopped walnuts
2 1/4 cups flour
1 teaspoon baking soda
1 teaspoon baking powder
1/2 teaspoon salt

TOPPING:
1 teaspoon butter, melted
1/3 cup sugar
1 teaspoon cinnamon

IN LARGE BOWL, combine brown sugar, oil, egg, vanilla, black walnut flavoring, and buttermilk. Stir in rhubarb and walnuts. In a separate bowl, stir together flour, baking soda, baking powder, and salt; then stir into wet mixture. Do not overmix.

Spray muffin pan with a non-stick spray and fill 3/4 full with batter. Mix topping ingredients together, and sprinkle over tops of muffins. Bake in a preheated 350 degree oven for 20 minutes or until toothpick inserted in the middle comes out clean. Makes 12 muffins.

Norma Peters
TALL FIRS GARDEN

---

succession planting

Succession planting helps to make the most use of your soil's fertility. Once nutrient-rich compost, aged manure, or other fertilizer is added into the soil, there is a natural succession of plants that should follow each other.

Lead the way with heavy feeders like celery, broccoli, corn, lettuce, or squash. Once the heavy feeders have been harvested, follow them with light feeders such as carrots, potatoes, onions, or beets. Many light feeders frown on excess nitrogen and will benefit when a heavy feeder, like squash, precedes it.

Now it's time to feed nutrients back into the soil. You can do this by planting crops that actually improve the soil like peas, beans, clover, fava beans, or vetch. Succession planting is ideal for continuous growing and harvesting, and for gardeners with limited space.

Rhubarb Swirl

Another delicious way to serve rhubarb

3 cups rhubarb, diced
3/4 cup sugar
1 3-ounce package strawberry Jello
1 regular size box (3.4 ounce)
   instant vanilla pudding

1 1/2 cups milk
1/4 teaspoon vanilla
8 ounces cool whip
1 9-inch graham cracker crust

MIX RHUBARB and sugar together in a sauce pan; let stand for 1 hour. Bring to boil, then simmer until tender. Stir in Jello, remove from heat and cool until syrupy. In a medium bowl, prepare pudding according to package directions with milk and vanilla. When thickened, add cool whip and stir to combine.

Pour rhubarb mixture into pudding mixture and gently swirl. Pour into crust or serve plain as pudding. Chill several hours. Serves 6 to 8.

Norma Peters
TALL FIRS GARDEN

Cooked Apple Cake

It's ironic—David and Pamela Rosenquist live right next to a nature trail. No wonder they started making bird houses and named their business "For The Birds". Now they market their houses at the Belfair Farmers' Market, and personalize each birdhouse with humor and puns to fit the owner.

This cake is one of my favorites and is a great way to use up some extra apples.

3 to 4 Braeburn apples*
1/2 cup butter or margarine
2 eggs
1 cup sugar
1/2 cup buttermilk, sour milk, or
   sour cream

1 teaspoon baking soda
1/2 teaspoon cocoa
1/4 teaspoon nutmeg
1/4 teaspoon cinnamon
1/2 cup chopped walnuts
1 1/2 cups flour

*Or substitute 1 cup applesauce instead

COOK APPLES with a little bit of water in a non-stick pan until tender. In a large bowl, cream together butter, eggs, and sugar. Stir in buttermilk and add cooked apple. Mix together remaining ingredients (except nuts) in a separate bowl, then add to wet ingredients, stirring to mix. Stir in nuts. Grease and flour a 9 x 12-inch baking dish; pour in batter. Bake in a preheated 350 degree oven for 40 minutes. Serves 12.

David & Pamela Rosenquist
FOR THE BIRDS

Strawberry Glace Pie

Diane Keith, once known as the Berry Lady Of Matlock for her tasty strawberries, has taken to making tool leather items these days. Keith, now known as The Leather Lady, sells buckskin suntops and other assorted leather items at the Belfair Farmers' Market.

When I started raising strawberries, this recipe became a favorite to all. Be sure to make two at a time, it goes fast! Try substituting raspberries or blueberries for a different taste.

1 9-inch graham cracker crust pie shell	3 tablespoons cornstarch
6 cups fresh strawberries	1/2 cup water
(about 1-1/2 quarts)	1 3-ounce package cream cheese, softened
1 cup sugar	

MASH BERRIES in a large bowl. Mix sugar and cornstarch in a 2 quart saucepan; gradually stir in water and mashed berries. Cook over medium heat, stirring constantly, until mixture thickens and boils. Boil for 1 minute. Allow to cool.

Beat cream cheese until smooth. Spread on bottom of pie shell, then fill shell with cooled berry mixture; refrigerate until set. Serve chilled. Top with cool whip if desired. Serves 6 to 8.

Diane Keith
THE LEATHER LADY

---

raspberry roundup

Fresh raspberries may have lots of Vitamin C and only 65 calories in each cup, but they weren't always valued for their delicious tasting fruit. Plants and berries have been used in healing for more than 2,000 years.

The true medicinal value of raspberries was disclosed in a 1941 study published by the British Medical Journal, Lancet. It seems raspberry leaves contain a uterine relaxant principle which may be helpful during childbirth. There are also astringent tannins in those leaves, which are of value in treating diarrhea.

One thing is for sure, raspberries are an all-around tasty plant. The leaves make delicious tea, and the berries, well there's nothing like them. Those berries are also packed with lots of fiber as well as vitamins A and C.

And for those of you on a low-fat diet, you can enjoy that fantastic raspberry taste to your hearts content.

sources of dietary fiber	**Fruits**		**Vegetables**		**Grains, Beans & Nuts**	
	Food	*Fiber**	*Food*	*Fiber**	*Food*	*Fiber**
	Apple	2.4	Broccoli, fresh	3.9	Beans, kidney, cooked	10.4
	Blackberries	6.2	Carrots, fresh	3.3	Flour, 100% whole wheat	9.6
	Dates, dried	8.7	Corn, sweet, cooked	5.7	Lentils, cooked	3.7
	Pears	2.4	Peas, cooked	6.3	Nuts, almonds	14.3
	Prunes, dried	16.1	Spinach, fresh	3.5	Nuts, walnuts	5.2
	Raspberries	7.4	Spinach, cooked	6.3	Popcorn, popped	16.5
	Strawberries	2.2	Tomato, fresh	1.5	Rice, brown, cooked	2.4

* per 100 grams (one ounce equals 28.35 grams; 100 grams = approximately 4 ounces)

Summer Days Fresh Herbal Tea Blend

Winter Nights Dried Herb Tea Blend

Horseradish Salad Dressing · Red Pepper Pesto

Sandwich Glue · Spring Tonic Soup

Crabby Mikes Smoked Salmon Spread

Three Bean Salad · Cranberry Salad · Marinated Baby Corn

Dilly Beans · Oven Roasted Potatoes

Sesame Noodles with Edamame · Tamale Bean Pie

Yummy Bean Casserole · Fresh Seafood Fettuccine

Crabby Mikes Half Shell Oysters · Cheese Sticks

Focaccia · Rising Corn Bread · Health Pancakes

Berry Muffins · Apple Dumplings

Cold Bread Pie · Cranberry Apple Cake

GRAYS HARBOR FARMERS' MARKET

LOCATION:
1956 Riverside Dr., on Highway 101
Year Round
Tuesdays, Thursdays, Fridays & Saturdays, 9:00 a.m.- 6:00 p.m.

WITH ITS FIRST STEPS, GRAYS HARBOR FARMERS' MARKET BEGAN AS A PARKING LOT Saturday market back in 1974. Today it has blossomed into a thriving indoor/outdoor year round farmers' market for all to enjoy. In fact, every year customers pin their home location on the market's map of the United States. By the end of the year, most of the states have been pinned along with many other countries!

It's no wonder the market draws so many visitors. Located on the banks of the Hoquiam River, the market is the perfect spot to shop before heading out to the Ocean Beaches and Rainforest on the Olympic Peninsula. There is a walkway along the river, playground equipment where kids play, and picnic tables to leisurely enjoy many of the market's delicious foods.

Several vendors provide live entertainment with their on-site production of foods and creative crafts. During crab season you'll experience the fresh flavor of live crab cooked in giant vats. Painters and wood carvers are usually at work, there are fresh baked goods prepared right at the Market, and even a vendor that makes fresh pasta. Crabby Mike makes homemade soup on Market days and has become famous for his weekend chowders.

The Market is abundant with fresh locally grown produce in the summer and fall, spring brings herbs and plants, then there's the wonderful winter selection perfect for holiday shopping of specialty crafts and baked goods.

There's something for everyone, including honey, jams, vinegars, baked goods, herbs, seafood, soups and salsas, plants, flowers, and books by local authors. Perhaps your interests lean more towards the spectacular artwork on canvas, saws, milk cans, and greeting cards. Quilts, wooden toys, bird houses and feeders, hand-made furniture, pottery, dolls and wreaths all make great gifts too.

Summer Days Fresh Herbal Tea Blend

"Herbs for the body and local fine art for the spirit" is the essence behind Kitty Mady's Roseworks Botanicals. Kitty offers a concoction of healing products including herbal teas and medicinals, sugar free jellies, "Dream Teddy's" sedative herbal pillows and more at Grays Harbor Farmers' Market.

Use fresh herbs for any or all of the following and dry the surplus for later.

1 cup raspberry or strawberry leaves
1 cup summer mint (peppermint,
    spearmint, etc.)
1 cup lemon balm or lemon verbena

1/2 cup chamomile flowers
1/2 cup fir needle tips (1-inch of new
    growth)

USE THE EQUIVALENT of 2 teaspoons fresh herb for each cup of tea, and steep, off the stove, for 5 minutes. Serve hot or cold. Add rose petals and lavender for color, sparkling water for a summer zinger, or honey to taste.

Kitty Mady
ROSEWORKS BOTANICALS

Winter Nights Dried Herb Tea Blend

Herbs should be dried before measuring. Keep the surplus in an airtight container for later use.

1 cup mint
1 cup lemon balm
1/2 cup purple clover heads
1/2 cup catnip leaves

1/4 cup rosehips
1/4 cup nettle leaves
1/8 cup cinnamon stick pieces

MIX ALL TOGETHER AND steep 1 teaspoon of the dried herb mixture in 1 cup water for 5 minutes. Strain and serve. I recommend this blend for colds, flu, or sore throat. Mixes well with apple cider or brandy.

Kitty Mady
ROSEWORKS BOTANICALS

Horseradish Salad Dressing

"Before I saw our home I had a dream. In my dream I saw the big fir trees, the yard and the little creek flowing through the area." That was nearly 30 years ago when Leona Auer found that dream farm. Soon, Al Strong, Leona's stepson, and his wife, Ruth, moved in and helped turn that dream into the vision it is today. Look for them and their fine assortment of familiar (spinach, lettuce, beets, leeks, beans) and not so familiar (zucchetta squash, purslane, poke, sorrel) produce at Grays Harbor Farmers' Market.

Deliciously smooth and creamy dressing with just the right amount of bite.

1/4 cup peeled and grated horseradish
2 cups mayonnaise
1/2 cup sour cream
1/3 cup buttermilk
1/4 cup oil

1/2 teaspoon onion powder
1/2 teaspoon salt
1/4 teaspoon black pepper
1/2 teaspoon kelp powder
1/8 cup vinegar

BLEND EVERYTHING well in blender or food processor until smooth. Keep refrigerated.

Ruth Strong

Red Pepper Pesto

Verona Latta first began growing and using herbs in her Connecticut home during the 50's. Now known as "The Herb Lady", Verona and her husband, Bear, started up Bears Herbs, Hearts & Flowers. They sell over 700 varieties of herbs, plus succulents, vegetables, everlastings, perennials, and a variety of seasoning blends, cranberry products, mustards, chutneys, vinegars, salsas, syrups, jams, and jellies. A tantalizing list of goodies which they bring to Grays Harbor Farmers' Market.

Classic pesto heats up with new zeal from red peppers. Toss with cooked linguini, add to your favorite soup, or spread on bread and broil.

1 15-ounce can red peppers, drained and rinsed
1 cup fresh basil leaves
1 8-ounce package cream cheese
1 teaspoon garlic
Salt and pepper to taste

PUT ALL INGREDIENTS in a food processor and blend for 1 minute or until creamy. Keep unused portions refrigerated.

Verona Latta
BEARS HERBS, HEARTS & FLOWERS

Sandwich Glue

Butter your sandwiches with this "glue" and the innards won't slip and slide.

1 8-ounce package cream cheese
1/4 cup Cranberry Mustard*
1 tablespoon Bears Ranch Dipper*

*Available through Bears Herbs, Hearts & Flowers at Grays Harbor Farmers' Market.

MIX ALL INGREDIENTS together in a small bowl till blended. Keep refrigerated.

Verona Latta
BEARS HERBS, HEARTS & FLOWERS

flowers you can eat

Did you know that nasturtiums can add a zing to salads, daylilies can be eaten like fritters, and borage flowers can refresh your iced drinks with a cooling cucumber taste? Edible flowers are making their appearance in more menus of restaurants and home kitchens than ever before.

First, be sure that a flower is edible before you decide to use it. Verify the Latin name, then look it up in any of the books recommended in the "Book Resource" chart. Second, always be sure to only consume pesticide-free edible flowers. Use pesticide-free edible flowers that you've grown yourself or bought at your local farmers' market or specialty store.

Sample the flower first before you add it to your dish. Some flowers have stronger tastes than others and may not appeal to you or your family. And finally, add edible flowers to a hot dish or beverage at the very last minute. Why not try out some of the unique flavors from the following edible flowers.

Anise Hyssop (*Aqastache Foeniculum*) - Strong anise taste, use sparingly.

Apple Blossom (*Malus spp.*) - Delicate floral taste.

Arugula (*Eruca sativa and E. selvatica*) - Creamy white flowers taste mildly of sesame and almonds. Delicious in salads and sprinkled over stir-fry.

Bee Balm/Bergamot (*Monarda didyma*) - With a taste reminiscent of citrus, bee balm gives color and zip to salads, curry dishes, salsa, chili, or even just floating in a punch bowl.

Borage (*Borago officinalis*) - Beautiful starry blue flowers with refreshing cucumber flavor.

Calendula (*Calendula officinalis*) - Mild flavor with slight delicate floral taste. Petals give nice saffron color to foods.

Chives (*Allium schoenoprasum* and *A. tuberosum*) - Pink flower petals hint of mild onion. White flowers of Chinese chives have a mild garlic taste. Use when buds first open.

Daylily (*Hemerocallis spp.*) - Taste varies among varieties; opt for floral and pleasant.

Spring Tonic Soup

Serve this delicious soup full of fresh springtime vegetables; hot, as a plain cream soup, or add leftover rice or pasta.

2 small potatoes
2 carrots, cut in large pieces
1 cup mixed broccoli and cauliflower florets
1 small onion

1 clove garlic
1 handful mixed young dandelion and
   nettle* greens
2 cups water

* Be sure to wear thick gloves and harvest carefully with scissors—nettles can sting!

STEAM ALL BUT the greens in pan until almost done; add greens during the last few minutes of cooking. Add cooked vegetables and stock to blender; puree on medium until smooth. Season to taste with any of the following: tamari, soy sauce, spirulina, Brewer's yeast, salt, pepper, butter, or cayenne.

Kitty Mady
ROSEWORKS BOTANICALS

---

more flowers you can eat

Fennel (*Foeniculum vulgare*) - Flowers from all culinary herbs are edible, with fennel flowers having a slight licorice flavor. Other interesting herb flowers to try are basil, rosemary, sage, and thyme.

Lavender (*Lavandula angustifolia*) - English lavender is best for cooking with its superior sweet lemon-floral taste. Also use in jams or to flavor vinegars.

Nasturtium (*Tropaeolum majus*) - Watercress flavor, somewhat spicy or peppery. Most commonly used flower and quite versatile.

Pinks (*Dianthus spp.*) - Delicate clove-like flavor, good in baked goods, fruit pies, iced and hot drinks.

Rose (*Rosa spp.*) - Flavors can vary from a rich, strong floral taste to slightly metallic. Remove the bitter white heel at the base and sample first.

Scarlet Runner Bean (*Phaseolus coccineus*) - Nice bean flavor that compliments many foods.

Squash Blossom (*Cucurbita spp.*) - A hint of squash flavor in a beautiful trumpet-shaped flower that's ideal for stuffing.

Viola and Pansy (*Viola cornuta, V.X. Wittrokiana*) - Delicate, light floral taste brings a colorful addition to the salad bowl.

Violet (*Viola odorata*) - Highly scented with strong floral flavor. Crystallize to decorate cakes, puddings, and ice cream.

Book Resources for Edible Flowers:

Sturtevant's Edible Plants of the World, edited by U.P. Hedrick (Dover Publications, 1972)

The Oxford Book of Food Plants, by G.B. Masefield, M. Wallis, S.G. Harrison, and B.E. Nicholson (Oxford University Press, 1975)

Edible Flowers, by Claire Clifton (McGraw-Hill, 1984)

Crabby Mikes Smoked Salmon Spread

Talk about a presentation of perpetual cuisine—Crabby Mikes Seafood-Pasta-Deli will reel you in—hook, line, and sinker! Michael Weiner and Joy Taylor entice you with fresh cooked crab, an assortment of seafood, and fresh pasta—all cooked on site. They also offer bavarian sausage, wild mushrooms, fresh pesto, soups, salads, and cheesecake at Grays Harbor Farmers' Market.

Salmon will always be an eternally unforgettable taste of the Northwest.

    1 16-ounce package cream cheese
    1 16-ounce container sour cream
    1/2 teaspoon MSG substitute
    1 4-ounce package Cajun Smoked Salmon by Briney Sea, broken in pieces
    1 small bunch fresh chives, diced

COMBINE IN BLENDER, cream cheese, sour cream, and MSG substitute; whirl till smooth. Add salmon and blend again till smooth. Transfer to a serving bowl, add fresh chives and stir to combine. Serve with crackers and enjoy.

Michael Weiner
CRABBY MIKES SEAFOOD-PASTA-DELI

Three Bean Salad

Serve with a side of fresh sliced tomatoes and basil. Absolutely delicious.

    1 16-ounce can kidney beans   1 large onion, minced
    1 16-ounce can green beans   1/3 cup sugar
    1 16-ounce can garbanzo beans   1 green bell pepper, minced
    1/2 cup oil   1 teaspoon ground black pepper
    1/2 cup vinegar

RINSE AND DRAIN beans; put in serving bowl. Add rest of ingredients to beans; toss lightly to mix. Store in refrigerator till ready to serve. Serves 4 to 6.

Ruth Strong

---

baby corn

Baby corn, produced from regular corn plants, is harvested early while the ears are very immature. Baby corn is easy to prepare and store, plus it adds a colorfully diverse appearance to vegetable dishes.

Unhusked baby corn can be stored in the refrigerator for up to one week without losing its crispness and flavor. Husk and wash baby corn, then steam for 5 minutes. Add baby corn to your favorite stir-fry recipe, pasta salad, or green salad. Also excellent marinated and served as a side dish.

Shaffner Farms

Cranberry Salad

This delicious blend of fresh cranberries, orange, and walnuts is especially enticing when served with chicken or turkey.

2 cups fresh cranberries
2 apples, cut in bite-size pieces
1 orange, peeled and seeded

2 cups sugar
1/2 cup chopped walnuts

PUT ORANGE SECTIONS in blender till juiced. Add cranberries and grind till semi-smooth. Pour into dish or serving bowl and add apples, sugar, and nuts. Refrigerate till ready to use.

Ruth Strong

Marinated Baby Corn

Family owned since 1977, Shaffner Farms is located in the Wynocchee River Valley outside of Montesano, Washington. Owen and JoAnn Shaffner sell a large assortment of produce like beans, edamame (green soybeans), corn, Asian vegetables, beets, carrots, pickling and slicing cucumbers, squash, pumpkins, and flowers. Their produce is available at their family farm stand, U-pick operation, and Gray's Harbor Farmers' Market.

Marinated baby corn can be stored in the refrigerator for several weeks.

2 pounds baby corn, husked and washed

Marinade
1 cup olive oil
1/2 cup cider or wine vinegar
1/4 cup lemon juice
1/2 teaspoon each salt and freshly
   ground black pepper

2 cloves garlic, pressed or minced
Pinch of 3 or 4 fresh herbs: marjoram,
   thyme, basil, dill, tarragon, parsley,
   oregano, chives

STEAM BABY CORN for 5 minutes or until tender. Drain and set aside. In a small bowl, combine all marinade ingredients and mix well. Place freshly steamed baby corn in a large glass jar or plastic container and cover with marinade, stirring to coat ears well. Serve warm or cold.

Owen & JoAnn Shaffner
SHAFFNER FARMS

Dilly Beans

Fresh and tender green beans with a touch of garlic, red pepper, and dill are "put up" for winter's use in an excitedly tasty way.

2 pounds fresh small tender beans
1 teaspoon red pepper
4 cloves garlic
4 large heads of fresh dill

2 cups water
1/4 cup pickling salt
2 cups white vinegar

PACK BEANS UNIFORMLY into hot sterilized jars. To each pint jar add 1/4 teaspoon red pepper, 1 clove garlic, and 1 head dill. Heat together water, salt, and vinegar; bring to a boil. Ladle hot liquid over beans, leaving a 1/4-inch head space. Remove air bubbles and seal. Process 10 minutes in a boiling-water canner. Yields 4 pints.

Owen & JoAnn Shaffner
SHAFFNER FARMS

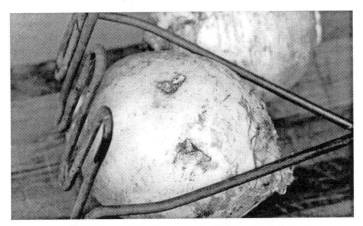

Oven Roasted Potatoes

Only organic flour and the best ingredients go into Nancy Lachel's baked goods. Nancy's Market Bakery has risen to new heights, or rather the delicious aroma of her fresh hot apple cinnamon rolls that she bakes on site has. Just follow your nose to a delicacy of specialty breads, pastries, pies, cookies, biscuits, jams, fresh salsas, spreads, cheese sticks and more at the Grays Harbor Farmers' Market.

Light and delicately roasted potatoes enhanced by onions and cheese.

4 to 5 pounds Yellow Finn potatoes
  (or your favorite variety)
1 cup chopped onions
1/4 cup tamari

8 tablespoons butter, melted
Black pepper to taste
Freshly grated parmesan cheese (optional)

PEEL POTATOES, cut into 1-inch chunks. Toss potatoes with onions, tamari, butter, and pepper in large bowl; transfer to baking sheet. Bake at 375 degrees for 1 hour, turning potatoes occasionally. Top with fresh cheese and serve.

Nancy Lachel
NANCY'S MARKET BAKERY

Sesame Noodles With Edamame

Sounds good!

Cooked edamame (pronounced ed-ah-mah-may) has a sweet nutty flavor, contains up to 40% protein, and is high in vitamin A, amino acids, and a wide range of minerals. In Japan, edamame are eaten as a snack with beer—much as Americans eat peanuts. Cooked edamame beans can also be added to any Asian-style dish. Only the bean is eaten, the pods are not edible.

Cooking: Add whole edamame pods to boiling water; salt is optional. Boil for 5 minutes. Drain the pods and serve warm. To eat the beans, lightly squeeze the pods and beans will pop out. Discard the pod.

1 pound Udon rice noodles*
1/2 cup sesame seeds
1/2 to 3/4 cup each: grated carrots,
    chopped broccoli, sweet red pepper
1 cup edamame, cooked and shelled
1/2 cup chopped green onion
1/2 cup brown rice or cider vinegar
1/4 cup tamari or soy sauce

2 to 3 tablespoons honey
2 cloves garlic, pressed
2 tablespoons peanut butter
1 tablespoon grated fresh ginger root
1/2 cup olive or other vegetable oil
3 tablespoons hot pepper sesame oil**
2 teaspoons orange zest (optional)
1/2 cup Mandarin oranges (optional)

* Or substitute linguini
** Or substitute 1 tablespoon crushed red pepper

PREPARE PASTA according to package instructions. Drain and set aside to cool. Toast sesame seeds in an oven or dry roast in skillet. Lightly steam broccoli. In a large bowl, toss together cooked pasta, broccoli, carrots, red pepper, green onions, edamame, and sesame seeds.

To make dressing, combine vinegar, soy sauce, honey, garlic, peanut butter, ginger, orange zest (optional), and oils; whisk together. Mix in dressing with pasta and orange sections (optional), tossing well to coat vegetables. Let stand 15 minutes to allow flavors to combine. Serve at room temperature. Serves 4 to 6.

Owen & JoAnn Shaffner
SHAFFNER FARMS

---

what is a cultivar

A combined form of the words "cultivated" and "variety", a cultivar can be a plant that has been produced through selective breeding. This is often done to produce a variety that may be more disease-resistant, perhaps a different color, tastier, bigger fruits and flowers, or just different, but hopefully better. But that's not to say that a cultivar is always better than the original species. A tomato may be more disease-resistant, but at a cost to the original flavor or some other desirable trait.

A new cultivar is given a number to identify it until that cultivar has been grown out and tested. Then once it makes it through that hurdle, it's given a name, then offered for sale in catalogs and at garden centers. A cultivar is not necessarily a hybrid.

Nature may also play a role in producing cultivars when two plants cross by chance and then a plant collector makes the discovery. Cultivars definitely have a place in any garden right along with heirlooms and old-fashioned varieties that are loved and grown through the centuries.

Tamale Bean Pie

Bring a taste of the South right into your own kitchen.

2 tablespoons oil
1 medium onion, chopped
1 clove garlic, minced
1 16-ounce can tomatoes, undrained
1/2 cup chopped green pepper
1/4 cup chopped ripe olives

2 teaspoons chili powder
1 15-ounce can pinto beans, rinsed
   and drained
1/3 cup grated Monterey Jack or
   Cheddar cheese

HEAT OIL IN skillet. Sauté onion and garlic till golden, about 10 to 15 minutes. Add remaining ingredients except beans and cheese; simmer uncovered 10 to 15 minutes. Add beans and set aside.

Cornmeal Crust
3/4 cup cornmeal
2 cups milk
2 teaspoons oil

1/2 teaspoon salt
2 eggs, lightly beaten

Mix cornmeal with 1/2 cup milk and oil; set aside. Heat rest of milk with salt in saucepan till it begins to simmer. Slowly add cornmeal/milk mixture, stirring constantly till thick and bubbly; about 5 minutes. Remove from heat and quickly stir in eggs.

Spoon half of crust mixture in bottom of greased 9 or 10-inch square baking dish. Cover with bean filling, then with remaining crust. Sprinkle top with 1/3 cup cheese. Bake at 375 degrees for 35 minutes or until heated through. Serves 4 to 6.

Ruth Strong

Yummy Bean Casserole

Perfect for an evening barbecue, potluck, or family picnic.

1 large can B & M Baked Beans
1/2 cup Cranberry Salsa*
1/4 cup minced onions**

2 tablespoons Cranberry Mustard*
1/4 cup dark molasses

* Available through Bears Herbs, Hearts & Flowers at Grays Harbor Farmers' Market.
** Or substitute 2 tablespoons minced dried onions

PLACE ALL INGREDIENTS in a Dutch oven; stir to combine. Bake at 300 degrees for up to an hour or until bubbly. Serves 4.

Verona Latta
BEARS HERBS, HEARTS & FLOWERS

Fresh Seafood Fettuccine

Seafood lovers will enjoy this gourmet fare of lobster, scallops, and prawns swimming in creamy sauce splashed with fresh herbs.

1 pound Crabby Mikes Fresh Fettuccine
1/4 pound scallops
1/4 pound prawns
1 small lobster tail, peeled and cut
   into 1-inch pieces
2 cloves garlic, minced

2 tablespoons butter or margarine
3 cups cream sauce (for a lighter sauce, use
   1 cup cream and 2 cups chicken stock)
1 teaspoon fresh chopped basil
1 teaspoon fresh snipped rosemary

BOIL WATER IN A LARGE POT and cook fettuccine until al dente. Sauté scallops, prawns, and lobster in butter or olive oil till almost done, then add garlic. Toss cooked fettuccine with seafood, fresh herbs, and cream in a large serving bowl. Serves 6.

Joy Taylor
CRABBY MIKES SEAFOOD-PASTA-DELI

Crabby Mikes Half Shell Oysters

I invented this recipe when I was Chef of Lake Cushman Resort in Mason County.

12 medium-sized oysters
1 cup bay shrimp, finely chopped
12 button mushrooms, finely chopped
1/2 cup dungeness crab meat,
   finely chopped
1/2 ounce cooking sherry

1/2 cup heavy cream
2 egg yolks
Pinch of salt and pepper
1 cup rock salt
1 cup grated Gruyere cheese
Paprika

SCRUB OYSTERS WELL. Shuck oysters over saucepan, saving oyster liquid and shells. Cook oysters over medium heat in their own juice until nearly cooked but firm. Remove oysters from saucepan and set aside.

Simmer shrimp, mushrooms, and crab meat in oyster juices until mushrooms are cooked, about 3 minutes. Add sherry and stir. Over low heat, slowly whisk in heavy cream.

In separate bowl, whisk egg yolks till smooth. Slowly add small amount of sauce from pan into egg yolks while continually whisking, then slowly whisk egg yolk mixture back into saucepan. Heat must be very low or egg yolks will curdle. Add pinch of salt and black pepper.

Arrange oyster shells on bed of rock salt. Place oysters in shells. Spoon sauce over oysters and sprinkle with cheese and paprika.

Michael Weiner
CRABBY MIKES SEAFOOD-PASTA-DELI

Cheese Sticks

This French bread dough is seasoned with dill weed, rosemary, and sun-dried tomatoes, then rolled in grated cheddar cheese and baked. Try this with sandwiches, along with a meal, or even by itself.

3 cups warm water
2 tablespoons honey
2 1/2 tablespoons yeast
4 cups unbleached flour

4 teaspoons salt
2 tablespoons canola oil

1/2 teaspoon dried dill weed
1/2 teaspoon dried crumbled rosemary
1/4 cup chopped sun-dried tomatoes

4 to 5 cups unbleached white flour
Grated cheddar cheese

DISSOLVE YEAST IN WATER with honey. Add flour, dill, rosemary, and sun-dried tomatoes; beat with a wooden spoon until elastic. This is the sponge stage. Cover and let rise in a warm spot until double.

Add salt and oil. Gradually add flour until dough comes away from the sides of the bowl. Knead, adding flour as needed. Raise dough in oiled bowl in a warm place until double in size. Punch down and knead briefly to get air pockets out.

Divide dough into four sections. Roll each section into a log, and roll in some of the grated cheese. Cut each log into six pieces, then roll strips about 6-inches long. Roll in additional cheese.

Place strips several inches apart on cookie sheet. Let rise in warm room for about 10 minutes. Bake in preheated 425 degree oven for 12 to 15 minutes, or until cheese is toasty. Cool on racks and serve. Makes 24 sticks.

Nancy Lachel
NANCY'S MARKET BAKERY

---

potato pitches

"What I say is that, if a man really like potatoes, he must be a pretty decent sort of fellow." — A.A. Milne, *Not That It Matters* (1920)

"Be eating one potato, peeling a second, have a third in your fist, and your eye on a fourth." — Old Irish Proverb

"Human nature will not flourish, any more than a potato, if it be planted and replanted, for too long a series of generations, in the same worn out soil." — Nathaniel Hawthorne, *The Scarlet Letter* (1850)

"Potatoes on the table
To eat with other things,
Potatoes with their jackets off
May do for dukes and kings.
But if you wish to taste them
As nature meant you should,
Be sure to keep their jackets on
And eat them in a wood.
A little salt and pepper,
A deal of open air,
And never was a banquet
That offered nobler fare."

— Edward Verall Lucas (1868-1938)

Focaccia

A moist and light Italian flat round bread that is often made with herbs. Terrific with soup or salad.

1 tablespoon yeast
1 teaspoon honey
1 cup lukewarm water

3 tablespoons olive oil
3 to 3 1/2 cups unbleached white flour
2 teaspoons salt

Toppings:
2 to 3 tablespoons olive oil
Salt
Freshly grated parmesan cheese

Garlic granules
Basil

IN A LARGE BOWL, dissolve yeast in lukewarm water and honey. Let sit a few minutes until foamy. Mix in olive oil, salt, and enough flour to make a thick batter. Beat a couple of minutes and gradually add more flour so that dough comes away from the sides of the bowl. Knead about 5 to 10 minutes, adding flour as needed.

Place dough in an oiled bowl in a warm place until double in size. Punch down and knead briefly to get air pockets out. Roll out on a lightly floured surface into a circle about 1-inch thick. Place on an oiled cookie sheet and let rise till almost double in size.

Dimple the dough by pressing your fingertips in, about 1-inch deep and 1 1/2-inches apart. Spread 2 to 3 tablespoons olive oil on dough, filling dimples. Sprinkle with salt and top with garlic granules, parmesan cheese, and basil.

Let sit about 10 minutes. Bake in a preheated 425 degree oven for 20 minutes. Cool on a wire rack, or eat while still warm.

Variations:

• Season with different herbs such as rosemary, thyme, or an Italian blend.
• Try sprinkling on chopped onions, sun-dried tomatoes, or olives.
• Let your imagination run wild and come up with your own favorite toppings.

Nancy Lachel
NANCY'S MARKET BAKERY

raspberry review	Variety	Season Bearing	Comments
	Bababerry	Fall	Large, sweet with distinctive flavor
	Boyne	Summer	Developed in Canada, excellent yields
	Chilliwack	Summer	From British Columbia, large and sweet
	Fall Gold	Fall	Golden yellow berries, vigorous and hardy
	Goldie	Fall	Deep gold firm berries, superior quality
	Heritage	Fall	Adaptable to most growing areas, excellent taste
	Jewel	Summer	Large black berry and plant, quite delicious
	Kiska	Summer	Very hardy, no heavy flavor, just light and sweet
	Kiwi Gold	Fall	From New Zealand, yellow berries with great flavor
	Meeker	Summer	Very productive, superior flavor
	Royalty	Summer	Purple berries, great for jams and jellies
	Summit	Fall	Super productive, fine berry flavor
	Taylor	Summer	Delicious flavor, heavy producer and quite hardy

Rising Corn Bread

For a variation in color and taste, try this with blue corn meal instead.

2 cups corn meal
1 cup flour
1/2 teaspoon salt
1 teaspoon baking powder

1/2 teaspoon baking soda
1 package active dry yeast
1/4 cup melted butter
2 1/2 cups buttermilk, heated to lukewarm

IN A LARGE BOWL, mix together corn meal, flour, salt, baking powder, soda, and yeast; set aside. Add heated buttermilk and melted butter to flour mixture. Let rise in a covered iron skillet for 30 minutes in a warm place. Bake in a preheated 350 degree oven for 30 minutes or until done. Serves 6 to 8.

Ruth Strong

Health Pancakes

This is the recipe for a mix that my father created during World War II. It has been a family staple ever since.

1 egg, slightly beaten
1/2 cup flour
1/2 cup Health Pancake Mix*
1 cup buttermilk

2 tablespoons canola oil
1/2 teaspoon salt
1/2 teaspoon baking soda

* Health Pancake Mix is available at Grays Harbor Farmers Market.

MIX ALL INGREDIENTS together in a bowl. Ladle out onto a heated griddle and cook until lightly brown. Serve hot.

Verona Latta
BEARS HERBS, HEARTS & FLOWERS

GRAYS HARBOR FARMERS' MARKET

Berry Muffins

These muffins can be host to either fresh or frozen berries. They are even better with a mixture of different berries. A great combination is marionberries with raspberries. If using frozen berries, do not thaw berries or your batter will discolor.

2 eggs
2/3 cup honey
1/2 cup canola oil
1 cup plain yogurt
1 teaspoon vanilla
2 1/4 cups unbleached white flour
1/2 cup oat bran
1 teaspoon baking powder

1 teaspoon baking soda
3/4 cup coarsely chopped walnuts
1 heaping cup or more of any of the
    following berries: marionberries,
    blackberries,raspberries, blueberries,
    huckleberries
Whole nuts to garnish tops of muffins

COMBINE IN A LARGE BOWL, the eggs, honey, oil, yogurt, and vanilla. In a separate bowl, mix flour, oat bran, baking soda, baking powder, and walnuts. Fold dry ingredients into wet ingredients, adding berries as soon as almost mixed. Be careful not to over mix or your muffins will be tough and form tunnels.

Fill muffin pans about 2/3 full with batter. Garnish each muffin with a walnut. Bake in preheated 400 degree oven for 18 to 20 minutes or until done. Baking time depends on whether you use fresh or frozen berries.

Set on rack to cool. Makes 12 to 18 muffins depending on size of muffin pan.

Nancy Lachel
NANCY'S MARKET BAKERY

---

bee by products

Honey results from the involvement of 3 important players—the honeybee, nectar, and enzymes. Once the bees collect nectar, they begin to evaporate excess water from the nectar. Then gland enzymes go to work to change the nectar into honey. Once in the hive, the bees soon ripen the honey with ventilation provided by the fanning of their wings and warmth from the bees in the hive. The resulting product is a sweet, easily digestible food enjoyed by many.

Pollen is a highly nutritious food and is sold in many natural food stores. The pollen (male germ cells produced by plants) is collected by a pollen trap that the beekeeper has located at the entrance to the hive. The trap gathers the pollen before it is changed into honey. The removal of pollen from the hive can place stress on a colony since it is important to the hive's nutrition (especially young bees) by providing a source of protein and fat.

Royal Jelly is a high-protein food produced from glands in the heads of young worker bees. Sometimes called bee milk, this jelly is fed to queen larvae and active laying queens. Yellowish and milky in appearance, royal jelly is mostly water (about two-thirds), with the remainder being about 90% protein.

Propolis has a natural antibacterial effect and is often used in medicines. It is a collection of plant gums and resins, mixed with the bee's enzymes, wax, and pollen. Bees use propolis as a hive disinfectant and sealer for any cracks or crevices. Propolis also gives a varnish-like waterproof protection to the hive.

Beeswax contains about 300 components and is secreted by wax-producing bees that are usually two to three weeks of age. Used by bees to build honeycomb, it's been estimated that 8 to 16 pounds of honey are needed to produce just 1 pound of wax.

Apple Dumplings

These make a wonderful finish to a meal or as center stage for a special breakfast.

10 to 12 large baking apples
2 cups brown sugar
1 1/2 cubes softened butter or margarine
2 teaspoons cinnamon

1 teaspoon nutmeg
1/2 cup finely chopped walnuts
1 generous pie crust recipe of your choice

PEEL AND CORE APPLES. To make filling, combine sugar, butter, nuts and spices in a bowl. Press filling into the hollow center of each apple, patting any extra filling on the outside of apple.

Divide pie dough into 10 to 12 balls. Roll out each ball large enough to fold up and around an apple with enough extra to crimp, leaving about 1/2-inch on top. Place dough-covered apples a few inches apart in a baking pan.

Bake in a preheated 375 degree oven for 50 to 60 minutes. To test for doneness, pierce apple with fork; if tender then the apple is ready. Serve warm or cold. They reheat nicely and are great served with ice cream. Makes 10 to 12 dumplings.

Nancy Lachel
NANCY'S MARKET BAKERY

Cold Bread Pie

This dish was popular in North Carolina because it was easy to prepare and wild berries were readily available.

6 or 8 biscuits
Strawberries, blackberries, or raspberries; fresh or frozen
Sugar

SLICE BISCUITS AND BROWN in oven. Cook berries in a small amount of water and sweeten with sugar to taste. In a pan or bowl, place a layer of biscuits, then layer of fruit; repeat layers. Cover dish and let the pie set for up to an hour; serve cold.

Leona Auer

Cranberry Apple Cake

Forget stringing cranberries and popcorn. Start a new Christmas tradition with the tangy taste of cranberries baked into this spicy, scrumptious cake.

1/2 cup butter	2 cups flour
2 eggs	2 tablespoons cocoa
1 cup sugar	1 teaspoon cinnamon
1 1/2 cups unsweetened applesauce	1/2 teaspoon nutmeg
1 teaspoon vanilla	1/4 teaspoon each allspice & cloves
1 cup dried cranberries	1 heaping tablespoon baking soda
1 cup chopped walnuts	1 tablespoon water

CREAM TOGETHER butter, eggs, and sugar in a large mixing bowl; stir in applesauce. In a separate bowl, combine remaining ingredients; stir well. Gently fold in flour mixture to applesauce mixture until just combined. Pour in a prepared 9 x 13-inch baking pan Bake at 350 degrees for 45 minutes. Serves 8 to 12.

Verona Latta
BEARS HERBS, HEARTS & FLOWERS

bringing in beneficial insects

Beneficial insects do indeed seek out and destroy pest insects like aphids, caterpillars, spider mites, and leaf hoppers. No wonder they can be a gardener's best friend. Encourage them to stay in the garden by providing a continual supply of pollen and nectar for the adult beneficials. Grow their favorites such as any flowering member of the umbel or daisy (composite) family. Just think of any flower that is umbrella shaped like dill, fennel, parsley, coriander, angelica, and sweet cicely which invite good parasitic wasps, ladybugs, lacewings, hover flies, and other predator insects to the garden.

Larger predatory insects like ground beetles, ladybugs, and rove beetles visit flowers of the composite family. Think of daisy-like flowers with petals circling a round center. Echinacea, calendula, feverfew, goldenrod, zinnias, cosmos, African daisies, and of course, sunflowers are good examples. And don't forget about vegetables that have gone to flower. Corn, epazote, and flowering broccoli all provide a dinner haven for beneficials too.

Kiwi Lemon Jam

Spiced Blueberry Jam or Chutney

Mixed Bean Salad · Ginger Mustard Coleslaw

Tomato Fritters · Zucchini Relish

Swiss Chard & Tomato Frittata

Cauliflower & Pea Curry

Feta Swiss Chard Pizza

Spaghetti with Bacon and Peas

Easy "Sopapilla" with Green Tomatoes

Ratatouille · Spicy Sausage & Potatoes

Lemon Beef & Broccoli

Zucchini Bread · Fruit Coffee Cake

Hmm Good Cookies · Grandma's "Forgotten" Cookies

KINGSTON FARMERS' MARKET

LOCATION:
Kingston Marina Park
at the foot of the Kingston Ferry dock
May to Mid-October
Saturdays, 9:00 a.m. - 2:00 p.m.

THE KINGSTON FARMERS' MARKET IS WELL KNOWN FOR ITS PICTURESQUE SETTING AT THE marina, surrounded by pleasure boats, Puget Sound and the Olympic Mountains. Many local families, visitors and ferry travelers spend their Saturday mornings there, enjoying the sites, the market music, and doing their shopping at the 40 to 50 stalls. The shoppers and vendors are all relaxed and friendly at this weekly community gathering spot.

The Market got its start in 1990 with only 10 vendors. It still carries the same purpose as it did then—to provide a place for North Kitsap residents to buy fresh local produce and hand-crafted goods from the Kitsap and Olympic Peninsulas. Today the Market has grown to over 100 vendors on the roster, each committed to bringing quality goods, plants, food and produce, all hand-made or home-grown.

The fun never stops at the Market with weekly entertainment by local musicians. Special summer events have included art festivals, boating safety demonstrations, harvest festivals, library book sales, pie contests, gardening and cooking classes, and multi-cultural celebrations. The Market also coordinates with other community groups to help create major festivals like the Kingston Bluegrass Festival and the Kingston Fourth of July Celebration. Every week one booth space is donated to a local non-profit group such as 4-H Llama Love, Boy Scouts, Red Cross, and Habitat for Humanity.

The entertainment is fantastic fun, but the heart and soul of the market continues to be the wondrous array of things to buy. The beautiful and varied produce, a wide variety of plants and colorful cut flowers, luscious breads and pastries, and naturally the mouth-watering smells of fajitas, sausages and other cooked foods all take center stage. But they are surrounded by distinguished and varied crafts of all kinds that fit many tastes and pocketbooks. It's an enchanting spot to spend a summer Saturday!

Kiwi Lemon Jam

Dorothy and Jeff Thomas of D & J's Goods are among the original 10 vendors who started the Kingston Farmers' Market in 1990. They continue to be a "Backbone" and critical part of the market—they sell coffee! That's not all. They also have homemade jams (Jeff is well-known for his Captain Berry jams) and delicious cookies for both humans and dogs, plus lovely sewn hats, ear-warmers, and kitchen accessories.

Kiwis bring a refreshingly tropical tart/sweet taste to many foods, including jams.

3 pounds and 4 ounces peeled kiwi, crushed or shredded
3 medium lemons, yellow portion of peel plus juice

3 pounds and 14 ounces sugar
MCP pectin

PREPARE JAM using standard cooked jam recipe found on MCP pectin. Pour into hot jars and seal, processing in a boiling-water canner according to instructions. Makes 12 jars.

Jeff & Dorothy Thomas
D & J'S GOODS

Spiced Blueberry Jam or Chutney

Naomi Maasberg of Raven Woodworks creates fine furniture and wood accessories for the home or office. She specializes in earth-friendly woodworking using reclaimed lumber and sustainable harvested hardwoods. Naomi is Board Treasurer for the Kingston Farmers' Market.

The freshness of blueberries with just a hint of spiciness.

1 pound blueberries (2-1/2 cups crushed)
2 cups sugar
1 tablespoon lemon juice

1/2 teaspoon cinnamon
1/8 teaspoon cloves
1/2 of a 6-ounce bottle of pectin

IN A KETTLE, combine berries, sugar, lemon juice, and spices. Bring to full rolling boil and boil hard, uncovered, for 1 minute; stir constantly. Remove from heat and stir in pectin. Skim foam; pour into sterilized jars and seal. Makes 5 to 6 half pints.

Naomi Maasberg
RAVEN WOODWORKS

Mixed Bean Salad

Beatrice Idris of Raven Nursery brings a portable forest of stunning trees and shrubs to the Kingston Farmers' Market. She has been invaluable on the Board for several years, organizing children's markets, raffles, decorations for special events and more. Her daughters usually get involved too and have become dynamite raffle ticket sellers!

Use any combination of your favorite dried beans, or buy them already mixed.

3 cups dried mixed beans
12 cups water
1 tablespoon salt
1/2 pound salt pork, cut into
   1/4-inch cubes
4 red sweet peppers, diced

1/2 pound feta cheese
1 teaspoon ground cumin
1/2 cup chopped fresh cilantro leaves
1/4 cup olive oil
Salt, pepper, Tabasco sauce, spiced vinegar
   to taste

IN A LARGE POT, simmer beans in salted water until tender, about 1 to 2 hours. Drain, rinse, and let cool. Fry salt pork in a skillet until crisp; drain excess fat. In a large bowl, combine cooked beans, salt pork, and remaining ingredients; mix well. Serves 4 to 6.

Beatrice Idris
RAVEN NURSERY

---

garlic storage tips

Outside of winter squash, no other vegetable stores quite as well in its natural state as garlic. A prime head of garlic kept in the right conditions can sometimes keep up to a year. Three important factors determine garlic's storage life: the type of garlic, the appearance of the garlic before storage, and the conditions in which it's stored.

First you need to know if the garlic you're buying is a hardneck or softneck type. For long-term storage, choose softnecks. The storage life of a hardneck can vary from 2 months to 6 months. Under ideal conditions, some softnecks can keep up to a year.

Look for heads that are firm and free from any sign of mold or spoilage. The bulb should be intact and protected by the paper-like wrappers. Individual cloves do not keep well and neither does a bulb where the cloves are showing signs of separation. Stems should be cut within 1 to 2 inches of the bulb. A bulb with a part of the stem left will always last longer than one with the stem removed.

Store garlic in a cool (40 to 55 degrees), dry and well-ventilated place. Garlic should never be stored in the refrigerator.

Ginger Mustard Coleslaw

Known as "The Bread Lady" of the Kingston Farmers' Market, Eileen France of Sweets & Savories is an extraordinary baker of pastries and focaccia. She also bakes exquisite wedding cakes, caters gourmet meals, and teaches classes on cooking. Eileen has led the Board for years and makes sure the Kingston Market is well advertised throughout the county.

A crisp-textured coleslaw loaded with spicy mouth-watering flavor.

2 1/2 pounds shredded cabbage (1/2 head each red cabbage and bok choy)
1 red pepper, sliced into matchsticks
1/2 cup chopped scallions (green onions)
4 carrots, grated
1 small red onion, diced
3 tablespoons apple cider vinegar
3 tablespoons lemon juice

2 tablespoons Dijon mustard
4 cloves garlic, crushed
1 Jalapeno chile pepper, minced
2 teaspoons peeled and grated fresh ginger
2/3 cup olive oil
3 tablespoons minced cilantro leaves
Kosher salt
Freshly ground pepper

TOSS TOGETHER CABBAGE, red pepper, carrots and onions in a large bowl; set aside. Make dressing by whisking together the vinegar, lemon juice, mustard, garlic, chile pepper, and ginger. Slowly whisk in the oil; add the cilantro. Season with salt and pepper to taste. Pour dressing over cabbage mixture and toss until all vegetables are well coated. Let rest at least 10 minutes before serving, or cover and chill until ready to use. Serves 6.

Eileen France
SWEETS & SAVORIES

A Spring Reminisce

Oh spring, where is thy length?
Where is thy rain and thunder and light?
Thy floods and thy mud and hour of wishing for summer?

Gone is thee, away thou has fled.
Past is thy presence and forgotten is thy wet breeze.
Summer is nigh and has covered thy tracks.

Dry is the ground that I walk where thou once laid.
Gone are the nights waiting for you to seep in,
awakened by your sound.

Away you have flown,
disappeared in the blue sky of summer.
You have passed and I miss thee.

— Rick Wetherbee

Tomato Fritters

A regular at the Kingston Farmers' Market, Dick Meixner and his family entice everyone with samples from their Northwest Country Kitchens spicy chili, which they sell in dry mixes. They also have dry soup and spice mixes.

Rich tomato-flavored fritters goes beyond wonderful with fresh basil.

3 cups chopped fresh tomatoes*
1 cup all-purpose flour
1 teaspoon baking powder
1 teaspoon sugar
3/4 teaspoon salt

2 tablespoons fresh snipped basil
1 tablespoon finely minced parsley
1 tablespoon finely minced onion
1 egg, beaten

* Or substitute one 28-ounce can tomatoes seeded and chopped.

DRY TOMATOES on paper towels. Mix together all ingredients including tomatoes in a large bowl. Do not overmix. Preheat oil in a skillet to 360°F. Drop batter by rounded tablespoons into hot oil and fry until golden brown. Drain on paper towels and serve.

Dick Meixner
NORTHWEST COUNTRY KITCHENS

---

plant enemies

Just as some plant combinations make good neighbors, there are others that don't get along. Invasive plants should be separated from plants that they'll overtake. Other plant enemies compete for the same nutrients, or attract the same pests, providing an easy target for the bugs. Some plants release substances into the soil that can inhibit the growth of other plants.

Gardeners for centuries have observed this effect, though most have not been thoroughly tested. Watch your own garden, and if your seeds won't germinate or your plants are failing and you've exhausted all other possibilities, consider the plant growing next door.

PLANT	KEEP AWAY FROM	PLANT	KEEP AWAY FROM
Beans	onions, garlic, shallots, leeks	Peas	onions, garlic, shallots, leeks
Beets	pole beans, mustards		
Broccoli	strawberries, sunflowers	Peppers	eggplant, tomatoes, potatoes, fennel
Cabbage	strawberries, grapes, sunflowers	Potatoes	eggplant, peppers,
Carrots	dill	Potatoes	tomatoes, squash, pumpkins, sunflowers
Corn	tomatoes, sunflowers		
Eggplant	potatoes, tomatoes, peppers	Strawberries	cabbage family
		Tomatoes	corn, potatoes, peppers, eggplant
Garlic	beans, peas		
Lettuce	cabbage family, sunflowers	Turnips/	mustards, cabbage
Onions	beans, peas	Rutabagas	family

Zucchini Relish

With her farm just 3/4 mile from the Kingston Farmers' Market, Joleen Palmer of Palmer Gardens brings organic produce, including her gourmet salad greens mix that has become legendary and is in high demand. She also produces fresh, fruity salad dressings that double as glazes and sauces for vegetables and meats.

This zucchini relish is a nice change of pace to standard cucumber relishes.

10 cups shredded zucchini, seeded with skins	2 1/2 cups vinegar
4 cups chopped onions	1 teaspoon turmeric
1/2 pound green peppers, chopped	2 tablespoons cornstarch
1 sweet red bell pepper, chopped	1 tablespoon nutmeg
5 tablespoons salt	1 tablespoon dry mustard
6 cups sugar	2 teaspoons celery seed
	1/2 teaspoon alum

PLACE ZUCCHINI and other vegetables in large bowl (not aluminum), sprinkle with salt and let stand overnight. Drain off juices, cover with water to rinse; drain again. Put well-drained zucchini along with sugar and rest of spices in a large pot or kettle. Cook gently for 30 minutes. Ladle into hot canning jars while boiling, and seal. Process in a boiling water canner for 10 minutes. Makes 14 half pints.

Joleen Palmer
PALMER GARDENS

seasoned potatoes

Do your potatoes tend to sprout early or even rot in storage long before you have a change to use them? A group of Greek scientists have discovered a group of herbs that curb sprouting potatoes and inhibit bacteria that cause them to rot. Researchers tested the essential oils of lavender, sage and rosemary along with their dried counterparts against a control group of potatoes that were kept in the same conditions, minus the herbs.

We tested this method for ourselves, storing one group of potatoes with rosemary, some with sage, and some without any herbs at all. When we checked our potatoes in the spring, we found the "herb potatoes" to have far fewer sprouts and less rotting than the unseasoned group. But don't worry, your potatoes will still taste like potatoes.

Swiss Chard & Tomato Frittata

Marcia Adams of Rainshadow Farm is another of the originators of the Kingston Farmers' Market. She continually has the largest produce stand under her familiar green umbrella along with a large assortment of organic produce. She also raises sheep and is a very busy sheep shearer in the county. Marcia keeps bees and brings her wonderful fresh local honey as well as the beekeepers associations' for an annual demonstration.

Topped with grated Parmesan cheese, frittata unfolds into a fresh garden medley of tomato, Swiss chard, and basil.

1 pound Swiss chard	3 tablespoons chopped fresh basil
4 cloves garlic, minced	1/4 teaspoon salt
1 cup chopped onions	1/4 teaspoon ground black pepper
2 teaspoons olive oil	1 medium tomato, sliced
6 egg whites	Freshly grated Parmesan cheese
2 whole eggs	

WASH THE SWISS CHARD, remove and discard the large stems (ribs); finely chop the leaves. In a 10 to 12-inch nonstick skillet, sauté the garlic and onions in 1 teaspoon of the oil for 3 minutes on medium heat. Add the Swiss chard, stir, cover, and lower heat. Cook about 10 minutes. Remove skillet from heat and drain the Swiss chard if juicy.

In a large bowl, beat the egg whites, whole eggs, basil, salt and pepper until blended. Stir in sautéed Swiss chard. Coat the bottom of skillet with remaining teaspoon of oil; return to medium heat. When the skillet is hot, pour in the Swiss chard-egg mixture; arrange tomato slices on top. Cover and cook for 5 to 8 minutes or until the edges are firm and the bottom is golden and beginning to brown.

Place a large, flat plate or pizza pan over the skillet and flip the skillet over so that the frittata falls on the plate. Slide the frittata back into the skillet and cook for about 5 minutes or so until the eggs are fully cooked. Serve immediately.

Marcia Adams
RAINSHADOW FARM

Cauliflower & Pea Curry

A creamy delight with the fragrant seasoning of curry. Serve with whole wheat chapatis or pita bread.

1 medium head cauliflower, cut into florets
2 medium potatoes, scrubbed and cubed
2 tablespoon butter
1 medium onion, chopped
1 1/2 tablespoons curry powder
1 1/2 teaspoons grated fresh ginger

1 teaspoon cumin seed
1/4 teaspoon hot pepper flakes
2 cups unflavored yogurt
1 tablespoon cornstarch
2 cups fresh shelled peas, sugar snaps or
    snow peas, cut into small pieces

STEAM CAULIFLOWER and potato until just crisp-tender, 8 to 10 minutes. Drain. Meanwhile, melt butter in large Dutch oven over medium heat. Add onion and sauté until transparent and soft. Add curry powder, ginger, cumin, and hot pepper flakes. Stir for 1 minute. Mix yogurt with cornstarch, then stir into curry mixture. Add cauliflower, potatoes, and peas. Heat until all vegetables are heated through but still crisp tender. Serves 4 to 6.

Marcia Adams
RAINSHADOW FARM

Feta Swiss Chard Pizza

A unique twist on an old favorite.

1 prebaked pizza shell

Topping:
10 ounces fresh Swiss chard; rinsed,
    stemmed and coarsely chopped
1 tablespoon olive oil
1 teaspoon dried dill
1 cup ricotta cheese

1/2 cup chopped scallions
1 cup crumbled feta cheese
Dash of ground black pepper
2 tomatoes thinly sliced, or 6 cherry
    tomatoes cut in half

SAUTÉ SWISS CHARD in oil on high heat for several minutes until just wilted. Drain the cooked chard in a colander or sieve, pressing out excess moisture with the back of large serving spoon. In a large bowl, combine topping ingredients (except tomatoes). Place the pizza crust on an unoiled baking sheet. Spread on the topping, arrange tomato slices on pizza, and bake in a preheated 450 degree oven for 10 to 15 minutes or until the cheese is bubbling and the crust is crisp. Serves 4 to 6.

Marcia Adams
RAINSHADOW FARM

Spaghetti with Bacon and Peas

Tender fresh snow peas in a creamy cheese sauce served over spaghetti.

1 pound thin spaghetti or vermicelli
4 slices bacon
1 medium onion, finely chopped
1-1/2 cups peas, either sugar snap peas
    or snow peas
1 15-ounce container part-skim ricotta cheese

1/2 cup grated Parmesan or Romano
    cheese
1/2 teaspoon salt
1/4 teaspoon pepper

IN A LARGE SAUCEPOT, prepare pasta in boiling salted water as label directs. Meanwhile, in a 12-inch skillet, cook bacon over medium heat until browned. Transfer to paper towels to drain. Pour off all but 1 tablespoon bacon fat from skillet. Add onion; cook until tender and golden. Steam peas until tender (7 to 10 minutes for sugar snap peas, 10 to 15 minutes for snow peas) and add to onion mixture.

When pasta is cooked, remove 1 cup pasta cooking water. Drain pasta. Return to pot and toss with ricotta, Romano, salt, pepper, and reserved pasta cooking water. Add onions, peas, and crumbled bacon; toss again. Serves 4.

Marcia Adams
RAINSHADOW FARM

scallion versus the green onion	The term "scallion" and "green onion" are often used interchangeably. To some, a scallion is a green onion, but a green onion isn't always a scallion. Though to serious cooks there is a difference. Scallions have a delicate flavor found only in a non-bulbing type of onion such as Lisbon or Evergreen White Bunching. For a green onion, any onion will do as long as it's harvested while the bulb is still small and immature.
	Although there may be a difference between the two in definition and sometimes in taste, that difference ends when it comes to selecting them. Look for tender green tops that show no signs of yellowing. Bulbs should be 1/2-inch or less in diameter with thin and tender skins. Use green tops and bulbs in salads, dressings, soups, stir-fry, and sauces.

Easy "Sopapilla" with Green Tomatoes

Hearty Mexican filling served "enchilada style".

1 cup cubed chicken or pork
1 tablespoon oil
2 cloves garlic, minced
Salt to taste
2 to 3 tablespoons flour
4 green chiles, seeded and sliced

2 to 3 cups cubed green tomatoes
Tortillas
Shredded cheese, cheddar or jack
Sour cream
Guacamole

BROWN CHICKEN OR PORK in oil with garlic and salt. Drain off excess oil and add flour to coat the meat. Add chiles and enough water to make it a little runny. Add green tomatoes and cook until heated through and thickened. Serve sauce in warm tortilla with shredded cheese, sour cream, and guacamole on top.

Naomi Maasberg
RAVEN WOODWORKS

blackberry pickin'

Those of us that love blackberries are lucky to live in an area where they grow wild and in abundance. Two introduced species that now commonly grow wild are the Himalayan Blackberry and Evergreen Blackberry. Usually ripening first, the Himalayan blackberry is quite juicy and sweet. The evergreen blackberry is not quite as juicy but the flavor tends to be more developed. Blackberry season may vary depending on your location, but generally begins in late July and lasts through September.

Be ready to "gear up" when picking blackberries. The thorns are quite sharp! Heavy-duty long pants, a long-sleeved shirt and gloves on one hand can save a lot of wear and tear on you. The ultimate gear though includes heavy boots (to move into the patch), and a bucket tied to your waist. After all, both hands need to be free; one to grab the vine and the other to pick berries!

Besides lots of taste, blackberries also have plenty of fiber, minerals, B vitamins and vitamin C. Look for berries that have no trace of red on them. If there is, they will be tart! Shiny black berries may also be tart and not yet ripe. When the berry begins to lose its gloss and pulls easily from the vine, it will be at its berry best.

Refrigerate berries immediately and wait to wash until you are ready to use them. Berries also freeze well by placing a thin layer of berries on a cookie sheet. Once individually frozen, they're ready to put in freezer bags or containers.

Ratatouille

Tom Stoner, head chef at Kingston Thriftway, is a master chef and a graduate of the Culinary Institute of America. He graciously was loaned to the Kingston Farmers' Market for our Harvest Festival last year and demonstrated several recipes one can make with the local produce available at the market. The samples were divine!

Brimming with zucchini, eggplant, tomatoes, herbs, and garlic, this rustic Provencal vegetable casserole may be served at any temperature and has a tendency to improve in flavor over time.

2 teaspoons extra-virgin olive oil
5 ounces red onion, medium diced
3/4 ounce garlic, minced
5/8 ounce shallots, minced
1-1/2 ounces tomato paste
8 ounces zucchini, seeded and diced medium
7 ounces red bell pepper, medium diced
7 ounces eggplant, peeled and medium diced

5 ounces yellow summer squash, seeded and medium diced
2 cups chicken stock
16 ounces plum tomatoes, peeled and thickly sliced
2 tablespoons chopped fresh basil
2 teaspoons chopped fresh oregano
1/2 teaspoon kosher salt, or to taste
1/4 teaspoon ground black pepper, or to taste

HEAT OLIVE OIL and add the red onion, garlic, and shallots. Sweat until onions are tender and translucent. Add the tomato paste and sauté until mixture develops a sweet aroma and rusty color.

Add the zucchini, peppers, eggplant, yellow squash, tomatoes, and stock. Bring to a boil; stir often. Reduce heat to simmer and continue cooking until eggplant is soft and vegetables are tender. Stir in the basil, oregano, salt and pepper. Serve or chill till ready to use. Serves 4.

Tom Stoner, Head Chef
KINGSTON THRIFTWAY

Spicy Sausage & Potatoes

Lisa Marcotte is one of our "junior" vendors, a teenage entrepreneur. She is a great baker and sells giant cookies and other treats. Her mom, Sue, comes with her and knits on her knitting machine to the fascination of many customers.

New red potatoes and spicy sausage create a winning combination for a quick skillet meal.

1-1/2 pounds mild Italian sausage
   (about 6 links) cut into 1-inch pieces
10 small new red potatoes, quartered
1/2 teaspoon pepper

1/2 teaspoon thyme leaves
1 cup thinly sliced red onion
1/4 cup chopped fresh parsley
1 green pepper, cut into 1-inch pieces

IN A LARGE SKILLET, combine sausage, potatoes, pepper, and thyme. Cook over medium high heat, stirring occasionally until potatoes are browned, about 10 to 12 minutes. Reduce heat to low, cover, and cook until potatoes are tender, about 8 to 10 minutes more. Stir in remaining vegetables and cook, uncovered, until vegetables are crispy tender. Remove to a serving platter and enjoy. Serves 4 to 6.

Sue Marcotte

| **what is intensive planting** | Used is Europe for generations, intensive planting is also known as French intensive planting. This method uses wide mounded beds with plants spaced closely together to give you more production in less garden space. |

In conventional row gardening, single long rows are planted with wide aisles in between each row. The downside to this method is wasted space with more weeds and moisture loss. With intensive gardening, seeds or starts are planted closely in lines that go across the wide beds rather than in straight, single rows. Spacing in between the rows should also be as close. The width of the bed should be wider than with row planting, but narrow enough so that you can easily reach the center from either side (usually 3 to 4 feet).

When vegetables, herbs, and flowers are planted close together, they form a canopy over the soil as they grow. This reduces moisture loss, prevents temperatures extremes, and blocks out necessary light for any new emerging weeds, thus reducing the amount of time you spend weeding. The plants become, in effect, a living mulch for the soil. Plus, you'll get increased production from a smaller area which also means less watering.

The raised mounds or beds allow the soil to warm up quicker and drain better, so you can plant earlier. This close-crowded planting uses more nutrients than with plants spaced further apart, so it's important to add in lots of organic matter and nutrients to the soil.

The square foot method is similar, but instead of mini-rows within the beds, the garden is built in a series of squares that are 12" x 12" wide. For example, a 4' x 4' bed would have 16 squares. Each square is then planted intensively with seeds or plants spaced the same distance apart. In one square foot you could grow 16 carrots, 9 beets, 4 lettuce, or 1 tomato plant.

Lemon Beef & Broccoli

Tender sirloin steak is marinated in an enchanting blend of lemon and ginger.

1/4 cup butter or margarine
3 cups broccoli florets
1 medium onion, thinly sliced
3/4 teaspoon ginger
1/4 teaspoon salt
1/4 teaspoon pepper
1 tablespoon lemon juice

1 tablespoon Worcestershire sauce
1 teaspoon minced fresh garlic
1 pound beef sirloin steak, cut into thin
  strips
2 medium ripe tomatoes, cut into 1-inch
  pieces

MELT BUTTER in a skillet until sizzling. Sauté broccoli and onion until crisp tender, about 5 minutes. Meanwhile, make marinade in a medium size bowl by stirring together remaining ingredients, except steak and tomatoes. Add sirloin strips; let stand 5 minutes. Add steak and marinade to vegetable mixture in skillet. Cook, stirring occasionally until meat is browned, about 7 minutes. Stir in tomatoes. Cover, then let stand until heated through. Serve over rice. Makes 4 servings.

Sue Marcotte

Zucchini Bread

See pg 12

Simply delicious!

3 eggs
2 cups sugar
1 cup oil   *m|t c*
2. — 3 teaspoons vanilla   *1 tsp*
2 cups peeled and shredded zucchini
3 cups flour

2 tsps — 1 teaspoon salt
1 teaspoon baking soda
3 teaspoons baking powder
1/2 teaspoon cinnamon   *— 3 tsps*
1 cup walnuts, chopped

add 2 T cocoa
1 c chopped dates

BEAT EGGS IN LARGE BOWL and add sugar, oil, and vanilla. When mixed, add zucchini. Stir in flour, salt, soda, cinnamon, baking powder and nuts. Fill greased and floured bread pans (4 small or 2 large) and bake in a preheated 350 degree oven for 45 minutes or until done.

Joleen Palmer
PALMER GARDENS

Fruit Coffee Cake

This is a family recipe I've been making since I was little. It's easy, very moist and delicious. Freezes well too, so you can bake lots when fruit is fresh and in season.

2 cups flour
1-1/2 cups sugar
2 teaspoons baking powder
1/2 cup margarine
2 eggs

1 teaspoon vanilla
3/4 cup milk
Fresh plums, apples, peaches, bananas, strawberries or other in-season fruit

WORK FLOUR, SUGAR, baking powder and margarine into crumbs in a mixer or food processor. Set aside 1 cup for topping. Add eggs, vanilla, and milk; mix well. Pour batter into a greased and floured pan.

Arrange sliced fresh fruit on top; be generous. Cover with crumb topping. Bake at 350 degrees for 45 minutes or until done.

Naomi Maasberg
RAVEN WOODWORKS

Hmm Good Cookies

One of our favorite recipes, this comes from Our Savior's Lutheran Church, Bremerton, Cookbook by Virginia Metcalf.

1 cup sugar
1 cup brown sugar
1 cup butter or margarine
1 cup oil
1 egg
1 teaspoon salt
1 teaspoon baking soda

1 teaspoon cream of tarter
3 cups flour
1 cup Rice Krispies cereal
1 cup oatmeal
1 cup shredded coconut
1 cup chopped nuts, your favorite
1 teaspoon vanilla extract

MIX SUGARS, butter, oil, egg, salt, soda, cream of tarter, and flour together in a large bowl. Add remaining ingredients and mix until well-blended.

With your hands, roll into individual small balls. Place on cookie sheet and press each ball with a fork. Bake in a preheated 350 degree oven for 10 to 15 minutes.

Jeff & Dorothy Thomas
D & J'S GOODS

GRANDMA'S "FORGOTTEN" COOKIES

Tecla Legge was a regular and enthusiastic customer at the Kingston Farmers' Market, and was soon recruited to the Board. She now volunteers at the Market almost every weekend, works on advertising, and is writing the Market newsletter.

Simply heavenly, these light airy clouds with nutty sweetness are often called meringue cookies or "kisses".

2 egg whites
2/3 cup sugar
1 cup chopped pecans or almonds
1 cup chocolate chips or butterscotch morsels

BEAT TOGETHER egg whites and sugar in a medium bowl until stiff. Add remaining ingredients and stir. Drop by small spoonfuls on lightly greased cookie sheet. Put in a preheated 350 degree oven and immediately turn off the oven (keep oven door closed). Leave cookies in oven overnight. Makes 2 dozen

Tecla Legge

Catnip Tea ▪ Outstanding Apple Cider

Salal Berry Jelly ▪ Chocolate Raspberry Jam

Sweet and Sour Prune Sauce

Zucchini Relish ▪ Cheese

Sundried Tomato Pesto

Pickled Beets ▪ Parsnips

Meatless Minestrone Soup

Baked Winter Squash

Summer Squash Cheese Casserole

Sautéed Summer Squash

Orange Ginger Zucchini Bread

Roasted Sunflower Seeds

Homemade Dog Food

KITSAP REGIONAL FARMERS' MARKET

LOCATION:
Parking lot on Bay Street behind Peninsula Feed Store
Last week of April thru October
Saturdays, 9:00 a.m. - 3:00 p.m.

With a beautiful view of the harbor, the Kitsap Regional Farmers' Market is located on the waterfront just one block east of the Port Orchard Ferry. You can come by Ferry or by your own private boat and walk the one block to the parking lot next to the Peninsula Feed Store. First started on Fredericks Street back in 1978, the Market is home to nearly 80 farmers and crafters.

Being an open air market gives everyone a gorgeous scenic view that's unbeatable. You'll enjoy the live entertainment that strolls through the Market, giving your day a festive feel. Great fun for the whole family.

Four special events throughout the season will entice you with fantastic shopping. The first event, Plant Day, happens on the second Saturday of May, and this is the time to stock up on plants for the yard and garden. Berry Day occurs on the second Saturday of July when all the different varieties of berries are ripe, juicy and ready for your selection. The second Saturday of August blooms profusely with flowers galore, on—you guessed it—Flower Day. And the second Saturday of October features Apple Day, with every juicy crunchy bite that you would expect from this part of apple country.

Bring the family for a fun, entertaining, and relaxing time you'll always remember.

Catnip Tea

Once the site of an old sawmill, Hard Pan Hill has now become a productive market garden because of Ben and Carmen Davis. It wasn't easy to cultivate a lush garden on top of a hill with hard pan soil just 6-inches below in many places. But the last 22 years of using organic methods have created fertile grounds to grow an abundance of fruits and vegetables for the Kitsap Farmers' Market. Their pumpkins, Indian corn, and eggs have become their specialty.

As a parent with a lot of stress, one of my favorite remedies is homegrown herb teas. I find catnip tea to be especially relaxing and soothing. Mint tea is also good served hot or over ice, but don't steep it more than 10 minutes.

    1 teaspoon dried catnip buds and leaves
    1 cup water

If you have a tea ball made for one serving, fill it with the fresh picked leaf and bud of catnip, or use one teaspoon dried. Let steep about 15 to 20 minutes; sweeten to taste. Makes 1 cup.

Carmen Davis
HARDPAN HILL

garlic lovers guide	Variety	Description	Type
	California Early	Large with 12-18 cloves per bulb. Clove is tan or off-white. Commonly available in many food stores.	Softneck
	German Red	Large with 10-15 cloves per bulb. Hot and spicy cloves favored by chefs.	Hardneck
	Inchelium Red	Top rated softneck at Rodale's garlic taste test. Mild lingering flavor/taste sharpens with storage.	Softneck
	Italian Late	Long-storing, strong and pungent with excellent flavor.	Softneck
	Korean Red	Easy peel, large bulbs with 5-10 cloves. Purple-striped bulb wrappers. Very hot! Poor storing.	Hardneck
	Northern White	Potent cloves average 5-7 per bulb. Excellent for baking.	Hardneck
	Purple Italian Easy Peel	Rich, spicy flavor with sweet aftertaste. Large cloves peel easily and store well.	Hardneck
	Sicilian Silver	One of the best keepers. Strong flavor is great for cooking.	Softneck
	Silver Rose	Rose-colored cloves with a sharp flavor. Stores well.	Softneck
	Spanish Roja	Easy-peel, very popular. Rich, spicy true garlic flavor. Northwest heirloom.	Hardneck

Outstanding Apple Cider

We have been making cider for years and ours is the best I've ever tasted. We also brought our cider press to the Farmers' Market to help celebrate Apple Day by squeezing cider for the public. The E. coli threat caused us to be a lot more cautious about the apples we were squeezing for others and to help others learn how to avoid E. coli.

WHAT YOU WILL NEED:

Apples
Large stainless steel bowls
   that will fit under
   cider press to catch juice
Large buckets
Cheese cloth

Clothes pins
Cider Press
Jars, lids, rings
Canner
Thermometer

STEP ONE: Choose your apples carefully. We guarantee that if you make your cider using Gravensteins, Kings, or Northern Spy Apples, you will make outstanding cider. Throw out all rotten or badly damaged apples.

STEP TWO: Our local Health Department recommends coring all apples before putting them through the cider press. Because of the E. Coli problems that have been recently devastating our apple cider makers, we recommend that you pasteurize your cider before tasting it. If you pasteurize before you taste it, it won't matter whether or not you've cut or cored your apples.

If you are using a hand press like we do, you will need someone to put the apples through the grinder while you turn the handle. When the hopper is full of ground apples, set the press up to press. Cover your ground apples before squeezing with a board that fits perfectly into the top of the hopper. Make sure that you have a bowl ready to catch every drop of your juice.

When the bowl is full, quickly replace it with another bowl. Pour the cider through the cheese cloth that has been attached to a bucket with clothes pins. This will strain out the big chunks.

STEP THREE: From the bucket, ladle your cider directly into sterilized canning jars. I leave a one-inch head space. Clean the tops of each jar carefully before adding the lids and screwing down the rings.

Put jars of cider into the canner. Attach a thermometer to the inside of the pan. Heat the water to 185 degrees for 30 minutes. Remove the jars, tighten the lids and let cool. Any jar that doesn't seal should go straight to your stomach or the fridge.

Carmen Davis
HARDPAN HILL

zucchini — one size fits all?	As zucchini grows bigger, the texture and consistency change. Young zucchini is moist and tender, older zucchini has a more condensed flesh, is drier, and not quite as tender. For its tender best, choose zucchini while small, 4 to 8-inches in length. Zucchini bigger than that is best when sliced and roasted or broiled; cut in julienne strips for stir-fry; or shredded and baked into breads and muffins. Although, there is a size when zucchini is too big, then it's best used as a door stop or tossed into the compost pile. When it's difficult to cut through the skin with a sharp knife, then it's time to toss it out of the kitchen.

Salal Berry Jelly

In 1904, Carol Rodenberger's grandparents first settled in what was then known as 'View Park' in the Puget Sound area. A few things have changed since then. View Park is now Port Orchard, and Carol has moved in and started Carol's Kitchen Crafts. She grows an abundance of fruits, berries, and vegetables for her jams and jellies, and as produce for the Kitsap Farmers' Market.

Widely used by the coastal Indians as a staple in their diet, salal berries are black in color and about the size of blueberries.

3 cups salal berry juice
1/4 cup lemon juice
4 1/2 cups sugar
1 box MCP pectin

TO MAKE JUICE: Add 1/2 cup water to each 4 cups of salal berries; do not smash berries. Bring to a boil, let simmer 10 minutes or until juice flows freely from the berries. Strain juice through cheese cloth or jelly bag.

TO MAKE JELLY: Place juice in saucepan with pectin. Stir thoroughly to dissolve pectin. Bring to a boil; add sugar. Bring to a rolling boil and boil for 2 minutes. Ladle into hot 8 ounce jars and seal. Process in boiling water bath for 5 minutes. Yields 5 cups.

Carol Rodenberger
CAROL'S KITCHEN CRAFTS

Chocolate Raspberry Jam

This also makes an excellent ice cream topping.

5 cups raspberries, mashed
1 box Sure Jell Pectin
5 squares Bakers Unsweetened Chocolate
1/2 teaspoon margarine
7 cups sugar

IN LARGE SAUCEPAN, stir pectin into fruit; add chocolate and margarine. Bring mixture to full rolling boil, stirring constantly. Quickly stir in sugar and return to rolling boil for 1 minute. Remove from heat, ladle into hot jars and seal. Process in a boiling water bath for 5 minutes. Yields 9 cups.

Carol Rodenberger
CAROL'S KITCHEN CRAFTS

Sweet and Sour Prune Sauce

One year my husband and I picked 260 pounds of prunes to sell at the Market, but came home with 160 pounds still left. I started to make prune butter and it was the most sour prune butter I ever tasted. So I went with the idea of a sweet and sour sauce by adding garlic and soy sauce.

15 cups pureed cooked sour prunes
2 cups or more sugar (sweeten
    prune puree to taste)
2 cloves garlic
2/3 cups soy sauce

1 cup white vinegar
1/2 teaspoon salt
1/4 to 1/2 cup lemon juice
3 tablespoons cornstarch
1/2 cup water

SWEETEN PRUNE PUREE with sugar; adjust to taste. Add peeled whole garlic cloves to 1 cup prune puree in blender; blend until smooth. Add to original prune puree. Mix in soy sauce, vinegar, and salt. Add 1/4 cup lemon juice, then taste, adding more if needed. Simmer for 20 minutes. Blend cornstarch with 1/2 cup water, and slowly pour into simmering sauce; stirring frequently. Simmer 10 minutes more. Fill hot pint jars and seal. Process in boiling water bath for 10 minutes. Use on chicken, shrimp, pork, beef, or stir fry. Makes 8 pints.

Carmen Davis
HARDPAN HILL

Zucchini Relish

Having a glut of zucchini? No problem. Make up some relish and enjoy it all year long.

4 cups chopped zucchini, about 6 medium
2 cups chopped onions, about 2 medium
1 cup chopped green peppers
1 cup chopped red peppers
4 tablespoons salt

3 1/2 cups sugar
2 cups cider vinegar
4 teaspoons celery seed
2 teaspoons mustard seed

COMBINE ZUCCHINI, onion and peppers in a large bowl. Sprinkle with salt and cover with cold water. Let stand for 2 hours. Drain vegetables, press out any liquid. Combine remaining ingredients in a large pot and bring to a boil. Add vegetables and simmer for 10 minutes. Pack into hot pint-size jars, leaving a 1/4-inch head space. Process in a boiling-water canner for 10 minutes. Yields about 4 pints.

Carol Rodenberger
CAROL'S KITCHEN CRAFTS

Cheese

With 4 kids we could easily consume 4 gallons of milk a day, but since our cow gave 10 gallons a day, I had to come up with a way to use the surplus milk. I found a cheese recipe and started making cheese, and it wasn't long before I modified it to fit my own needs.

4 gallons of milk, 2 to 7 days old
   (my favorite is from a Guernsey
   or Jersey cow)
1 quart buttermilk
Rennet
9 x 12-inch cake pan

Salt
Vegetable steamer
Candy thermometer
Cake spatula
Cheese press

POUR FOUR GALLONS of two day old or older milk into a 5 gallon stainless steel pan. Add 1 quart of buttermilk; heat slowly to 90 degrees. Remove from heat and let set, covered, for 1 hour. Add in enough rennet for 4 gallons milk; mixing well. (I like the liquid drops but the tablets work fine. Each type of rennet has its own instructions. I located rennet in a health food store.) Let set 1 hour.

Heat back to 105 degrees while cutting the curd. (The white mass is the uncut curd. I use a long cake spatula to cut. The smaller you cut the curd, the drier the cheese will be.) Continue to stir until the desired temperature is reached. Once the temperature is reached, remove from heat and let the curd set one hour.

Drain the whey off of the curd. The curd should now be a solid mass on the bottom of the pan. (If the mass is on the bottom of the pan, you are well on your way to a good cheese. A floating mass won't make the best cheese, but it's still cheese.) Put the curd in a 9 x 12-inch cake pan and melt in the oven at 250 degrees for 30 minutes.

Salt and put the cheese in the cheese press overnight for a standard farm cheese. Salting the cheese is a variable. I always sprinkle about 3 tablespoons on the top before putting it into the cheese press. After you've made a few bricks of cheese you'll get to know how much salt you like. If you'd like to make Cheddar cheese instead, then read on.

I use my vegetable steamer to cheddar the cheese. Put the mass of curd into the steamer. Stick a candy thermometer into the mass; keeping the temperature between 110 and 115 degrees for 2 hours. Cut and turn the mass every 15 minutes for even cheddaring.

Put the mass of curd directly into cheese mold. Remove cheese the next morning. Eat your cheese whenever you'd like. If you want to age it, wrap it in a vinegar-soaked cloth and store in the refrigerator.

how to keep beets from bleeding	When it comes to bleeding beets, red is the runny culprit. You can help keep the red from bleeding into your other food with these tips.
	• Add a bit of lemon juice or vinegar to your cooking water the next time you throw in the beets. This helps to stabilize the red pigment and hold in that color.
	• When preparing beets, leave an inch of the leaf stalk attached to discourage bleeding.
	• If all else fails, use beets of a different color like gold or white.

Cheese Press

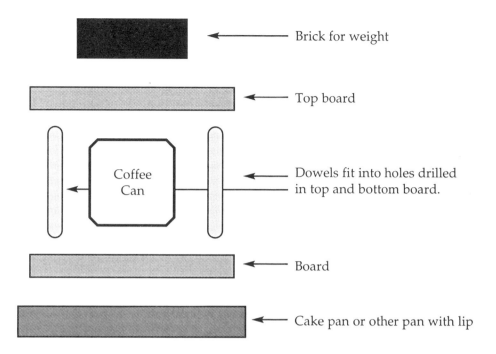

Brick for weight

Top board

Dowels fit into holes drilled in top and bottom board.

Coffee Can

Board

Cake pan or other pan with lip

The boards in my cheese press are very old pressboard, so I put a layer of wax paper below and above my cheese to keep it clean. If the cheese mass does not fill the coffee can, then I fill the empty space with a saucer and bowl or two. The idea is to put weight on the cheese and press it firmly into a shape while forcing the whey to drain completely out.

My mother-in-law recommends the brick. I've always used what was readily available, such as a bucket of peanut butter, a gallon of cooking oil, or anything that I could balance on my top board.

Carmen Davis
HARDPAN HILL

Sundried Tomato Pesto

Gold Mountain Herb Farm boasts one of the largest varieties of on-site grown herbs in Washington. John and Pamela Moyer are the fourth generation to live here, and they sell at the Kitsap Farmers' Market. Over 150 varieties of herbs are grown. They also offer fresh herbs, dried herbs, tea mixes, plus rare and endangered plants.

Great as a pizza topping, on crackers with cream cheese, tossed into salads, or baked into bread dough. Try it in soups and stews, or even stir into pasta.

2 cups sundried tomatoes packed in oil,
    drain and reserve oil
3/4 cup oil, preferably olive oil
1/2 cup fresh rosemary
1/2 cup fresh parsley

1/2 cup fresh oregano
3 to 5 cloves garlic
1/2 cup pine nuts or walnuts (optional)
3/4 cup shredded parmesan cheese

PROCESS ALL THE ABOVE ingredients except for cheese in food processor until smooth. Add cheese, mix well, and refrigerate up to 2 days. Can also be frozen.

Pamela Moyer
GOLD MOUNTAIN HERB FARM

Pickled Beets

Three generations now work to make Davis Farm what it is today. Famous for their green beans, beets, and pickling cucumbers, Davis Farm also brings a host of delicious produce to the Belfair, Gig Harbor, and Kitsap Farmers' Markets. You'll find a great selection including squash, corn, potatoes, strawberries, and raspberries, plus cut flowers, perennial plants, and eggs.

Pickling is a terrific way to extend the vegetable season throughout the year. If desired, you can omit the onions and substitute an additional 1 pound of beets.

3 pounds beets (about 24 small)
1 cup liquid, reserved from
    cooking beets
2 cups vinegar
1 cup sugar

2 tablespoons salt
6 whole cloves
1/2 pound onions, sliced
    (about 2 or 3 medium)

COOK BEETS until tender. Drain, reserving 1 cup of cooking liquid. Peel and slice beets. Combine all ingredients in a large kettle and heat to boiling; simmer 5 minutes. Pour into hot pint-sized jars, making sure liquid covers beets, and seal. Process in a boiling water bath for 5 minutes.

Irene Davis
DAVIS FAMILY FARM

Parsnips

The parsnips we grow are equally good, small or large. They especially seem to thrive for us. For a nice variation, try mashing them like potatoes, add butter and milk to taste.

4 to 8 parsnips
Butter to taste
Salt to taste

PEEL THE FRESH PARSNIPS and slice 1/4-inch thick. Put in a saucepan with enough water to cover the bottom of pan. Bring to boil, then cover and simmer for 8 to 10 minutes. Add butter and salt to taste. Serves 4 to 8.

Ben Davis
HARDPAN HILL

Meatless Minestrone Soup

Quick and easy fresh garden flavor. This soup also freezes nicely.

4 cups tomato juice
5 cups water
5 bouillon cubes
4 teaspoons dry minced onion
1 cup chopped celery
1/2 head cabbage, shredded

3 small zucchini, sliced
1 cup chopped mushrooms
1 teaspoon Italian seasoning
Dash garlic powder
Salt and pepper to taste

COMBINE ALL INGREDIENTS in a large pot, bring to a boil, then simmer for 1 hour. Serves 8 to 10.

Carol Rodenberger
CAROL'S KITCHEN CRAFTS

Baked Winter Squash

Pick your favorite winter squash for this recipe. A few suggestions are delicata, butternut, or buttercup.

1 winter squash
1/2 cup ham, cut into strips about
   1/4-inch wide by 2 to 3-inches long

1 tablespoon butter
1 clove garlic
Brown sugar

CUT YOUR FAVORITE winter squash in half; clean out strings and seeds. Rinse and lay face down on baking sheet. Cook in a preheated 350 degree oven for 30 minutes. Melt butter in saucepan and brown garlic. Remove the garlic and brown the ham strips. (You will need about 1/2 cup ham strips per 1 cup of hollowed space in squash.) Remove squash from oven; turn right side up. Cook for 15 minutes more. Fill squash halves with ham strips, dot with butter and sprinkle with brown sugar. Bake for 15 more minutes or until squash is done. Serves 2 to 4.

Carmen Davis
HARDPAN HILL

picking and storing winter squash

The term 'winter squash' can sometimes be misleading since it's usually harvested in late summer or early autumn. The term 'winter squash' comes about because with proper storage it can often be kept through winter. The ideal storage conditions are between 50 to 60 degrees with low humidity. A cool storage room, enclosed patio, garage, or unplugged freezer work well as long as it's not damp. Damp conditions will cause the squash to rot.

Keep the squash from touching each other and do not wash before storing. Here in the humid winter of the Pacific Northwest, smooth-skinned types like butternut or spaghetti keep better and store longer than bumpy skinned types like buttercup which gives a place for moisture to get in, causing mold and spoilage.

Winter squash will give you telltale signs when they are ready to be picked. Look for a subtle color change (depending on the variety), a stem that's slightly shriveled and brown, and a tough skin or rind that should not pierce easily with a thumbnail.

When selecting squash, look for those with good color (there should be no hint of green on non-green colored squash), and a nice firm skin or rind. Be sure the stem is 1-inch or longer if you plan to store your squash for any length of time.

Summer Squash Cheese Casserole

Use your favorite squash such as yellow crookneck, zucchini, or scallop.

2 to 3 pounds summer squash, sliced
1/2 cup water or broth
Salt and pepper to taste
3 tablespoons margarine

2 tablespoons flour
1/8 cup milk
1/2 cup grated cheese, your favorite
water

ARRANGE SUMMER SQUASH in a 9 x 12-inch casserole dish. Pour broth or water over squash, then salt and pepper to taste. Cover with foil and place in 350 degree oven for 20 minutes. While that is in the oven, melt margarine in saucepan and add flour; stirring quickly for 1 minute. Stir in about 1/4 cup water. When mixture thickens, remove from heat. Mix in milk and cheese; stir and add more water if necessary. Pour over casserole and cook for 10 minutes more. Serves about 6.

Carmen Davis
HARDPAN HILL

Sautéed Summer Squash

Use the young, tender squash for this recipe.

2 to 3 pounds small summer squash,
   sliced (yellow crookneck, zucchini,
   or scallop)

Margarine
 Seasoning salt to taste
Pepper to taste

HEAT A FRYING PAN on medium heat; add margarine. Toss squash into pan; add salt and pepper. Cook fast and eat hot! Serves 4 to 8.

Carmen Davis
HARDPAN HILL

Orange Ginger Zucchini Bread

Mary Lyons Felts grows all the berries for the pies she makes and sells at the Kitsap Farmers' Market. Just follow the aroma and that will lead you to Mary Lyons Felts Baking, where you'll also discover tempting breads, cookies, and cinnamon rolls.

The orange and ginger give an extraordinary twist to the ever popular zucchini bread.

3 eggs	2 cups shredded zucchini
3/4 cup oil	2 1/2 cups flour
1 1/2 cups sugar	2 teaspoons baking powder
1 teaspoon lemon peel	1 teaspoon baking soda
1/2 teaspoon orange extract	3/4 teaspoon salt
1/4 teaspoon vanilla	1/2 teaspoon ginger

BEAT TOGETHER in a large bowl the eggs, oil, and sugar. Add lemon peel, orange extract, vanilla, and zucchini; blend well. In a medium bowl, add the dry ingredients; stirring well. Add dry ingredients to wet ingredients, blending until just mixed.

Pour batter into 2 greased and floured medium loaf pans. Bake in a preheated 325 degree oven for 1 hour or until done. Makes 2 loaves.

Mary Lyons Felts
MARY LYONS FELTS BAKING

quotable honey quotes	"Eat honey, my son, for it is good." — King Solomon (Proverbs 24:13)
	"If you want to gather honey, don't kick over the beehive." — Abraham Lincoln
	"The use of honey is so soveraigne that nothing on our cold countries comes neare it for goodnesse and perfection..." — William Vaughn (Directions for Health, 1617)

Roasted Sunflower Seeds

Great snack to have on hand.

Sunflower seeds
salt
water

SOAK FRESH SEEDS for 3 to 5 hours in salted water. The ratio is anywhere from 1 to 2 teaspoons of salt per cup of water. Drain and lay the seeds on an absorbent towel for another 3 to 5 hours. Spread seeds on a greased baking sheet and put in a preheated 275 degree oven; leaving the door open about 1-inch for ventilation. Cook until desired crunch has been obtained. Cool, then store in an airtight container if there are any left.

Carmen Davis
HARDPAN HILL

what is a microclimate

A microclimate is a small area whose climate has been altered by the effects of environmental or man-made factors. Hills, trees, buildings, bodies of water, low-lying areas and windbreaks all influence microclimates. In your own garden and around your home you may experience microclimates that can have up to a 10 degree difference in temperature. That difference can be beneficial, or detrimental, to your plants.

Your microclimate can help you decide which plants to choose, and more importantly, where you will plant them. In a marginal climate, for example, a sun-loving fig tree will perform better if planted on the warm south side of a building or wall.

Pay attention to your yard on a frosty morning and note those areas showing more signs of frost. Areas near a building, porch, or over hanging eaves may show no signs of frost. Mapping out the microclimates of your yard can be the difference between success and failure for those tender "iffy" plants.

Homemade Dog Food

Kathy Parker sells soaps, skin creams, and skin care products through her mail-order catalog and at Kitsap Farmers' Market. She also teaches classes on how to make soap and skin cream.

This diet is especially good for older dogs with heart problems, but it's also a good diet for any healthy dog.

    2 to 3 cups cooked white rice (no salt added)
    1/2 pound regular (not lean) hamburger
    1 to 2 tablespoons oil (olive oil or wheat germ oil)
    1 complete dog vitamin

COOK HAMBURGER until juices run clear. Mix hamburger, cooked rice and oil together in a dog bowl. Feed with vitamin. A dog vitamin must be given once a day with this diet to prevent certain vitamin deficiencies. Feeds a 40 to 60 pound dog once per day.

Kathy Parker

---

new ways with mini pumpkins

Did you know that mini pumpkins also taste great? Cut off the tops and clean out the seeds just like you would for a jack-o-lantern. You can even get the kids involved and have them carve their own design.

Stuff with your favorite filling and bake in a 350 degree oven for about 1 hour. Stumped on which filling to use? Try any of the following combinations.

- ham, pineapple, honey, butter

- wild rice, bread crumbs, butter, rosemary

- apples (tart), brown sugar, butter, pecans, corn flakes

- marshmallow, butter, cinnamon

can you grow strawberries on a tree?

Though it doesn't actually grow strawberries, the Strawberry Tree (Arbutus unedo) does have tasty fruits that are somewhat savory like strawberries. The difference is that they are a bit drier and seedier than the more sumptuous, juicier strawberries.

The Strawberry Tree is not really a tree since it's slow growing and usually tops out at 10 to 20 feet. Tolerating temperatures as low as zero degrees, it can easily be pruned into a shorter shrub or to an open-crowned small tree. There are also cultivars of the Strawberry Tree that seldom get over 6 feet tall. The trunk, branches and even the stems of leaves tend to take on a beautiful reddish hue.

For color, edible fruits and a drought-resistant level of maintenance, it's hard to find a better choice than the Strawberry Tree.

Ed Reed's Southern California garden now totals over 400 different species of drought-resistant plants.

Bread and Butter Pickles

Jackie's Fresh Salsa · Salsa

Pesto Sauce

Mill Race Farm's Chard Soup

Zucchini Crisps

Vegetable Lasagne · Bean Hot Dish

Spaghetti with Sausage & Peppers

Biscuits · The Wonderful Waffle

Ginger Snaps · Orange Pineapple Muffins

Zucchini Buttermilk Bread

Applesauce Cake

Mill Race Farm's "No Fat or Low Fat" Fresh Apple Cake

Lemon Sponge Pie · Flat Apple Pie

KITTITAS COUNTY FARMERS MARKET

LOCATION:

Washington School, 5th & Anderson
May thru October
Saturdays, 9:00 a.m. - 1:00 p.m.

Every Saturday since 1994, people come from all around to browse, shop, and visit with friendly faces at the Kittitas County Farmers' Market. Located in an old school yard, there's plenty of room for lots of vendors and customers, plus a fun play area for the kids.

Most of the fresh produce you'll find at the Market is grown organically, and most of the Market season you can choose from plants and perennials of all sorts. There are always plenty of delicious baked goods, jams and jellies, cider, honey, and farm fresh eggs too. Brighten up your home or that of a friend with fabulous cut flowers and bouquets. And don't forget to check out the great array of hand made crafts including pottery, beadwork, wood crafts, fine arts, and clothing. You can learn how to prepare a new vegetable or custom order that special gift.

Come and experience all that the market is, rich in tradition and fun for the whole family. Enjoy all the makings for a meal that will long be remembered, a place to gather and meet the grower or crafter face to face, plus music, family activities, contests, grower workshops and more.

Bread and Butter Pickles

Katie Patterson of Katie's Ceramics sells finished ceramics, custom orders and "Paint Your Own" projects, bringing the project back glazed and fired the following week. This has proved to be particularly popular with young people and their parents. Look for her ceramics at the Kittitas County Farmers' Market.

This recipe comes from Granny Trimble's collection of recipes which were popular in her large extended family in the Texas Panhandle. Definitely a farming family!

1 gallon medium pickling cucumbers, sliced
4 small white onions, cut into narrow strips
2 green peppers, cut into narrow strips
2 red peppers, cut into narrow strips
1/2 cup coarse salt

1 quart cracked ice
5 cups white vinegar
5 cups sugar
1 1/2 teaspoons turmeric
1/2 teaspoon ground cloves
2 teaspoons mustard seed
2 teaspoons celery seed

PLACE CUCUMBERS, ONIONS and peppers in a large pot. Add salt, cover with cracked ice; mix well. Let stand for 3 hours, then drain. Combine other ingredients, pour over cucumbers. Bring to a boil. Pack into hot pint jars and seal. Process 10 minutes in a boiling-water canner. Yield: about 10 to 14 pints.

Katie Patterson
KATIE'S CERAMICS

Jackie's Fresh Salsa

Jackie Charlton of Jackie's Country Kitchen & Gardens helped start the Kittitas County Farmers' Market. Gardening for about 10 years, she grows organic produce including potatoes and beets. She also brings delicious garlic cheese breadsticks.

When you want your salsa to be really fresh, try this one-time serving salsa recipe with lots of flavor.

2 fresh tomatoes, chopped
4 fresh green onions, chopped
1 yellow onion, chopped fine
1 or 2 medium Jalapeno peppers, chopped fine

1 8-ounce can tomato sauce
2 tablespoons oil
3 tablespoons water
Salt & pepper to taste

MIX ALL INGREDIENTS together; add garlic powder to taste. Serve with chips and enjoy.

Jackie Charlton
JACKIE'S COUNTRY KITCHEN & GARDENS

Salsa

Established in 1988, Lori & Louise Becker have designed over 20 different items, selling both retail and wholesale. They bring handmade stuffed animals and baked goods, including their ever popular giant cookies, to the Kittitas County Farmers' Market.

This makes a large amount of salsa so you can have plenty to can and enjoy later on when fresh tomatoes are but a memory.

19 to 20 cups chopped tomatoes
3 medium onions, chopped
7 to 8 bell peppers, chopped
4 Jalapeno peppers, chopped
   (add more for a hotter sauce)
5 cloves garlic, minced

2 tablespoons salt
2 tablespoons chili powder
4 tablespoons parsley
1/2 tablespoon oregano
1 cup vinegar
12-ounce can tomato paste

COMBINE ALL INGREDIENTS together in a large pot; cook till boiling. Boil until desired thickness is reached. Pack into hot pint jars and seal. Process in a boiling-water canner for 20 minutes.

Lori Becker
RAINBOW'S END

heart smart oils

Fats can be found in many food sources like meats, dairy products, nuts, grains, and vegetables oils. Too much of some fats can be bad for your health, but there are actually "good fats" that can benefit our health. Fats contain both saturated and unsaturated (monounsaturated and polyunsaturated) fatty acids.

Saturated and trans fatty acids are the bad fats which can raise blood cholesterol levels that may lead to a heart attack. Animal and dairy products are usually high in saturated fats. When hydrogen molecules are added to polyunsaturated or monounsaturated fats, trans fatty acids are formed. These are found in partially hydrogenated vegetables oils like shortening and margarine.

The good fats help to reduce cholesterol and risk of heart attack when they supersede saturated fats we consume. Plus, they give our bodies lots of energy. Polyunsaturated fats are found in cold water fishes, most vegetables oils, and nuts. Monounsaturated fats are found in olive oil, canola oil, peanuts, and avocado. Here's a rundown of common cooking oils high in good fats. Amounts are listed in grams per tablespoon of oil.

Oils	Saturated	Monounsaturated	Polyunsaturated
Canola	1.0g	8.3g	4.3g
Corn	1.8g	3.5g	8.4g
Olive	1.9g	10.4g	1.2g
Peanut	2.4g	6.5g	4.5g
Safflower	1.7g	1.7g	6.2g
Sesame	2.0g	5.6g	5.9g
Sunflower	1.5	6.5g	5.7g

Pesto Sauce

Jerry Goronea and Anne Read began River Farm in 1977. Certified Organic Growers, they sell garlic (including garlic granules and powder), basil, tomatoes, melons, peppers, corn, cucumbers, pie cherries, apples and more at both Kittitas County and University District Farmers' Markets.

A rich hearty blend of fresh basil and parsley, olive oil, garlic, cheese, and nuts; especially good with pasta, on bread, or dolloped into soups and stews.

1 1/2 cups of tightly packed basil leaves
1/4 to 1/2 cup packed parsley leaves
1/2 cup grated Parmesan or
   Romano cheese

1/4 cup pine nuts*
4 cloves garlic, minced
1/2 cup olive oil**
2 oz. orange juice (see pg. 81)

* Or substitute sunflower seeds or walnuts instead
** Or use less olive oil and substitute with equal amount of water

COMBINE ALL INGREDIENTS except oil in blender or food processor; blend until smooth. Slowly drizzle in oil, scraping sides as needed, until blended. Keep refrigerated until ready to use (cover with small amount of olive oil). May also be frozen.

Jerry Goronea & Anne Read
RIVER FARM

Mill Race Farm's Chard Soup

Located in Thorp, Washington, Mill Race Farm is widely known for its registered Saanen dairy goats and fine hand-crafted Goat Milk Soap.

A hearty, satisfying soup with the fresh taste of chard and potatoes.

1 bunch (about 1 pound) Swiss chard
6 slices bacon, cut into 1/2-inch pieces
1 medium onion, finely chopped
4 cubes chicken bouillon

1 1/2 quarts water
2 1/2 cups diced potatoes
Salt and pepper to taste

WASH CHARD WELL; drain. Cut off and thinly slice the stems; separately slice the leaves. Set aside.

In a 5-quart kettle, fry bacon until crisp; lift out and drain. Discard all but 1 tablespoon of the drippings. Add onion to pan and sauté until limp. Stir in water, bouillon cubes, bacon, and potatoes. Cover and simmer 5 to 10 minutes, or until potatoes are almost tender. Add the chard stems and cook 5 minutes, then add the chard leaves and cook for 3 minutes longer. Season to taste with salt and pepper. Serves 6.

Dick & Ace Fields
MILL RACE FARM

Zucchini Crisps

10 years ago Joanne Taylor's husband built her a greenhouse so she could start plants for her garden. Now that garden has grown into Country Haven Gardens, producing 18 varieties of tomatoes, 22 varieties of peppers and lots of other produce for the Kittitas Country Farmers' Market. Joanne also brings lots of tomato, pepper, basil, and numerous herb plants as well as a variety of crafts.

Like magic, pounds of zucchini are turned into a tasty treat right before your eyes.

12 cups peeled and sliced zucchini
   (about 1/4-inch thick)
1 1/2 cups sugar
1 1/2 cups water

1/2 cup lemon juice
1 tablespoon cinnamon
3 tablespoons butter or margarine

BOIL INGREDIENTS TOGETHER (except butter) until zucchini is done. Add butter and pour into a 9 x 12-inch pan. Then mix together the following ingredients:

2 sticks margarine
2 1/2 cups flour*

2 1/2 tablespoons baking powder
1 1/2 cups brown sugar

* Or substitute 2 cups rolled oats and 1/2 cup flour

Pour over zucchini mixture. Bake at 350 degrees for 30 minutes or until brown and bubbly. Delicious!

Joanne Taylor
COUNTRY HAVEN GARDENS

I yam what I yam

Think you're buying yams in the supermarket? Well, think again. Even though they're advertised as yams, they're still sweet potatoes. Actually all of the varieties sold in supermarkets, whether labeled yams or sweet potatoes, are sweet potatoes. But don't let that stop you from buying those golden-brown or reddish-brown skinned beauties.

Forget the name and concentrate on the sweet, delicious taste sensation that can be enjoyed year-round in a variety of ways. Not only is it loaded with flavor, but it's also packed with a powerhouse of nutrients. In fact, the sweet potato has been rated as the #1 most nutritious vegetable according to the Center for Science in the Public Interest. Just one medium sweet potato is bursting with 26,082 IU of vitamin A, over twice the recommended daily allowance. Also an important source of beta carotene, the sweet potato only packs 140 calories and is fat-free.

Vegetable Lasagne

Green Acre Hobbies is a fitting name for the fresh garden produce and hand-crafted items grown and produced by Milly Bollinger and her husband Loran. Loran makes wood crafts and Milly does the painting or staining.

A low-fat pasta recipe with all the goodness of fresh farm produce for robust flavor.

2 teaspoons oil
3 cups unpeeled chopped eggplant
3/4 cup chopped onion
1 teaspoon minced garlic
1 28-ounce can crushed tomatoes
1/2 teaspoon sugar
1/4 teaspoon basil
1 pound peeled and shredded carrots

1 10-ounce package thawed frozen spinach
15 ounces ricotta cheese
1 cup shredded part-skim mozzarella cheese
1 egg, well beaten
Dash each of salt and nutmeg
1 package cooked lasagna noodles
Parmesan cheese

HEAT OIL IN SKILLET over low heat. Stir in eggplant, onion, and garlic; sauté for 5 minutes. Stir in crushed tomatoes, sugar, and basil. Add a dash of salt to taste. Cover and simmer for 20 minutes or till eggplant is tender.

Meanwhile, boil 2 quarts water and cook carrots 3 to 5 minutes. Drain well and add spinach, ricotta cheese, mozzarella cheese, beaten egg, dash of salt and nutmeg. Add eggplant mixture and stir to combine—this is your sauce. In a 9 x 12-inch baking dish, make layers of cooked noodles, then sauce, then repeat, ending with a last layer of sauce. Sprinkle parmesan cheese on top. Bake at 350 degrees for 30 minutes or till heated through. Serves 8 to 10.

Milly Bollinger
GREEN ACRE HOBBIES

selecting garlic stock	A bulb of garlic consists of individual cloves, each one producing a new bulb of garlic. So to get a great bulb of garlic at the end, plant good garlic from the start. Here are a few tips to keep in mind when selecting your planting stock.

- Big bulbs come from big cloves, so save your largest and best cloves for planting.

- Don't plant cloves from diseased stock. Use only unblemished, solid, and firm cloves.

- Be careful not to nick individual cloves when separating your bulb for planting. A simple nick can invite disease, especially in wet soil.

Bean Hot Dish

In Yakima valley, Annette and Travis Heine of The Giant Radish grow fruit and vegetables the natural way, without the use of harmful pesticides and chemicals. The Giant Radish also sells baked good such as fresh pies, fruit breads, cookies and candies along with jams and jellies at the Kittitas County Farmers' Market.

Even farmers' rely on quick meals they can throw together in an instant. This hearty bean dish will satisfy any hungry appetite.

2 pounds ground beef
1/2 cup diced onions
1 pound bacon, cut into small pieces
6 cups pork and beans
2 15-ounce cans kidney beans, drained
2 15-ounce cans lima beans, drained

1/2 cup brown sugar
2 tablespoons vinegar
1/2 teaspoon salt
1 tablespoon mustard
1 cup catsup

BROWN GROUND BEEF with onion in a roaster or large oven-proof pot; remove from pot. Fry bacon until crisp. Drain drippings from pot and add cooked ground beef and onions back to pot along with beans. Meanwhile, bring to boil in a sauce pan the brown sugar, vinegar, salt, mustard, and catsup. Add to beans in pot and bake, uncovered, at 350 degrees for 1 1/2 hours. Serves 4 to 6.

Annette Heine
THE GIANT RADISH

Spaghetti with Sausage & Peppers

As fresh as you can get, a full-flavored sauce that captures the essence of sun-ripened tomatoes.

1 pound sausage, cut into 1/4-inch slices
2 medium green peppers, thinly sliced
2 medium red peppers, thinly sliced
1 medium onion, thinly sliced
4 cups chopped tomatoes
3 cloves garlic, minced
6 to 8 drops hot pepper sauce

1 teaspoon paprika
1/4 teaspoon cayenne
2 tablespoons cornstarch
1/2 cup chicken broth
1 12-ounce package spaghetti noodles,
    cooked and drained

BROWN SAUSAGE IN a Dutch oven. Add peppers and onions; sauté 2 minutes. Add tomatoes, garlic, pepper sauce, paprika, and cayenne. Cook and stir until vegetables are tender. Combine broth and cornstarch, stir into sausage mixture. Bring to boil; cooking and stirring until thick. Add spaghetti and cook for 5 minutes more. Top with parmesan cheese if desired. Serves 4.

Joanne Taylor
COUNTRY HAVEN GARDENS

Biscuits

Here's the original recipe from Granny Trimble's collection. The "modernized version" follows.

Original Recipe

HAVE OVEN AT 450 DEGREES. Take lump of lard the size of an egg and place in baking pan, melt in oven. While lard is melting, put 1 cup buttermilk in bowl. Add one well rounded tablespoon of baking powder, 1/2 teaspoon of soda (more if buttermilk is very sour) and 1 teaspoon of salt; stir well. Add about 2/3 of melted lard. Add 2 1/2 small Pet milk cans of flour; dough will be sticky. Turn out on well-floured board and knead a few times until dough will stay together. Pat out to 1/2-inch and cut with Pet milk can. Dip tops in melted lard and place in pan. Bake until golden brown, about 10 or 15 minutes.

Modernized Version

1 cup buttermilk
1 1/2 tablespoons baking powder
1/2 teaspoon baking soda

1 teaspoon salt
2 or 3 tablespoons shortening
1 1/2 cups flour

MELT SHORTENING IN a 9 x 13-inch pan in hot (450 degree) oven. Add baking powder, soda and salt to buttermilk and stir; mixture will foam up. Add about 2/3 of melted shortening. Add flour and stir. Turn out on well-floured board and knead a little more flour in so dough can be handled without sticking. Pat dough out to 1/2-inch thick and cut with round cookie cutter. Dip tops of biscuits in melted shortening in pan and place in pan so they touch each other. This should make a full pan of biscuits. Bake at 450 degrees for 10 to 15 minutes or until golden brown.

Katie Patterson
KATIE'S CERAMICS

beet greens are tops	Hold on to those beet tops because they're packed with nutrition and flavor. With only half the calories, beet tops have more vitamins A, B1, B2, and C, plus more calcium and iron than the roots. Similar in taste to Swiss chard, the tender somewhat buttery texture of the tops are great in salads, lightly steamed or braised. If you like greens with a little less flavor intensity, use the tops from the gold or white beets instead.

The Wonderful Waffle

Barbara Owen of Ellensburg Pottery has been hand-crafting porcelain dinnerware and pots for plants since 1979. She also brings bird houses and feeders to the Kittitas County Farmers' Market.

Use a Belgian waffle iron to make this nutritious and colorfully delicious waffle for one.

1 egg
1 tablespoon yogurt
Milk
1 tablespoon whole wheat flour
1 tablespoon rice or quinoa flour
1 tablespoon buckwheat flour
1 tablespoon corn flour (not cornmeal)
1 tablespoon garbanzo bean flour or
   other bean flour

1/4 teaspoon baking powder
1/4 teaspoon salt
1 tablespoon ground-up nuts
   (pecans, walnuts, cashews, etc.)
An assortment of berries, bananas,
   and applesauce

IN A MEASURING CUP, add egg and yogurt with enough milk to make 2/3 cup of liquid. In a separate bowl, combine remaining ingredients; stir in liquid mixture. Pour into waffle iron and cook till done. Put on plate and put blueberries in some of the holes, raspberries in some of the holes, and hot applesauce over all. Add layer of cottage cheese, layer of yogurt, and top with strawberries and bananas.

Barbara Owen
ELLENSBURG POTTERY

Ginger Snaps

Spicy heart-warming cookies that are sure to become a family favorite.

3/4 cup shortening
1 cup brown sugar
1/4 cup molasses
1 egg
2 1/4 cups flour
2 teaspoons baking soda

1/2 teaspoon salt
1 teaspoon ginger
1 teaspoon cinnamon
1/2 teaspoon cloves
Sugar

MIX ALL INGREDIENTS TOGETHER, except sugar. Form into small balls, then roll balls in sugar. Place on greased cookie sheets. Bake in a preheated 375 degree oven for about 10 minutes. Let cool slightly, then remove from pan. Makes about 5 dozen cookies.

Annette Heine
THE GIANT RADISH

Orange Pineapple Muffins

Sweetened with orange juice and pineapple for a unbelievably tasty yet healthy muffin.

2 cups flour
3 teaspoons baking powder
1/4 teaspoon salt
3 tablespoons wheat bran
2 eggs
1 cup + 2 tablespoons orange juice
    concentrate

2/3 cup 2% milk
1/3 cup chopped walnuts
1 20-ounce can crushed pineapple,
    well drained

MIX DRY INGREDIENTS together in a bowl. In a larger bowl, mix eggs, milk, and orange juice concentrate together. Add the dry ingredients to the wet ingredients and stir just to combine. Fold in pineapple and nuts. Spoon batter into lightly greased muffin tins, about 3/4 full. Bake in a preheated 375 degree oven for 20 to 25 minutes. Makes 1 dozen.

Lori Becker
RAINBOW'S END

honey flavors

Honey can greatly differ in both color and flavor, depending on the source of nectar gathered by the honey bees. Colors can range from the nearly clear to midnight ebony, with most preferred honeys being a light to golden amber. Flavors can also vary from the delicately mild to fragrantly fruity to the distinctively bold.

Light colored honey is usually milder while the dark colored honey is stronger and more intense in flavor. Alfalfa, clover and wildflower are common honeys suitable for any use. Orange blossom or fruit honeys like blackberry are excellent with fruit or when used in baking. The intense flavor of the darker honey can be used as a marinade for meats or in barbecue sauce.

Alfalfa is ranked as the most important honey plant in Utah, Nevada, Idaho, Oregon and most of the western states. Alfalfa honey is white or extra light amber in color with a fine flavor. The honey also has a good body, which makes it the perfect table honey.

Blackberry is the primary honey in the Pacific Northwest and can make a light, golden-amber, or even ebony colored honey. The fruity, rich and full-flavored honey is slightly reminiscent of blackberries. An excellent all around honey and especially great for baking.

Clovers are the most popular honey plant in the United States. Depending on location and source, clover honey varies in color from water white to extra light amber and has a mild, delicate flavor. Clover honey is generally considered the standard for comparison.

Fireweed is a tall summer-blooming herb native to much of the Pacific Northwest. Light in color and mild in flavor, it is an excellent table honey.

Meadowfoam is unique to the Willamette Valley area of Oregon. Because of its intense and overpowering flavor, it's usually mixed with other honeys while in the hive. The resulting flavor is unrivaled, starting off light, followed by a cotton candy flavor, and then finishing with a hint of vanilla.

Mint creates a honey that is dark, rich and full-flavored. Referred to as "the stout beer of honeys", its flavor is not suggestive of mint at all. Its sweet honey flavor holds up well in baking and sauces, and it also makes a wonderful topping for waffles.

Orange Blossom honey is often a combination of citrus floral sources. It produces a white to extra light amber honey with a distinctive flavor and the aroma of orange blossoms. Although not a source in the Pacific Northwest, it is commonly available in stores throughout the country.

Poison Oak honey is surprisingly delicious. An excellent all around honey, some say it also improves resistance to Poison Oak. Production is found primarily from Yoncalla, Oregon and south. The flavor is light with nice floral tones, though not as light as clover.

Zucchini Buttermilk Bread

Zucchini pairs up with unlikely partners in this creative version. Onion, parmesan cheese and dill weed combine for a winning recipe.

1/2 cup melted butter
1 cup buttermilk
1/4 cup finely chopped onion
1 cup grated zucchini
2 eggs

3 cups flour
2 tablespoons sugar
1/2 cup parmesan cheese
1 tablespoon baking powder
1 teaspoon dill weed

COMBINE BUTTER, BUTTERMILK, onion, zucchini, and eggs in a large bowl. Mix dry ingredients in a separate bowl. Add to buttermilk mixture and stir until moistened. Pour batter in a greased and floured 9-inch deep dish pie plate. Bake at 350 degrees for 55 minutes. Serves 6.

Joanne Taylor
COUNTRY HAVEN GARDENS

corn-a-plenty

Maize, as corn was called long ago, comes in fascinating colors and varieties. Sweet corn is the type you eat on the cob or off and today comes in shades of white, yellow, orange, red (yes, red), or bi-colored.

Hooker's Sweet Corn came to this area nearly 70 years ago, named after Ira Hooker of Olympia, Washington. Eat it fresh when the kernels are a milky white or let it mature and dry to a blue-black color. It makes the sweetest cornmeal.

Field and/or flour corn goes by many names including starch, dent, ornamental corn and Indian corn. Colored kernels develop brilliant mixtures or solitary shades of pink, red, brown, blue, gray, black, yellow, gold, and purple. Use it for cornmeal or flour, decorating or animal feed. The young immature ears of some varieties can be eaten like sweet corn.

Another type of corn is popcorn. Not just any corn will pop. It needs to be an extra-hard form of flint corn. There are pink, white, and yellow varieties plus a multi-colored calico mix. But don't get too excited—the "popped" corn turns inside out and will not be the color of the kernel. Today popcorn is a popular snack food, but in colonial America is was eaten for breakfast with milk and maple sugar. Could this be the next breakfast of champions?

Applesauce Cake

This recipe makes a bread or cake which needs to be covered and kept for several days to be at its best. It makes a delicious holiday cake if chopped or cut dried fruits are added in addition to the raisins. For a richer cake, use plum puree instead of applesauce.

2 cups sugar
1/2 cup shortening
2 cups applesauce
3 cups all-purpose flour
2 teaspoons baking soda
1/2 teaspoon salt
1 teaspoon baking powder

1 teaspoon ground cloves
1 teaspoon cinnamon
1 teaspoon nutmeg
1 teaspoon vanilla
1 cup raisins (optional)
1 cup chopped nuts (optional)

CREAM TOGETHER SUGAR and shortening; add applesauce and stir to combine. Sift all dry ingredients together and gradually add to applesauce mixture. Add vanilla, then raisins and nuts if desired. Bake at 300 degrees for 1 hour or until done.

If cake will be eaten immediately, 1 egg should be added after the creaming step and before the applesauce. Frost with penuche or boiled caramel icing and wrap tightly. Also delicious basted with rum or brandy, then well-covered about a month before Christmas. In this case do not add the egg or the frosting.

Katie Patterson
KATIE'S CERAMICS

Mill Race Farm's "No Fat or Low Fat" Fresh Apple Cake

Nutritious and delicious with fresh apples, whole wheat, and yogurt. When pear season arrives, try substituting Bosc or Anjou pears for the apples for a change.

1 cup sugar
1 cup plain nonfat yogurt
3 eggs or equivalent egg substitute (egg substitute makes this recipe "no fat")
1 teaspoon vanilla
1 1/2 cups whole wheat flour

3/4 teaspoon cinnamon
1/4 teaspoon nutmeg
1 teaspoon baking soda
1 teaspoon salt
5 cups fresh apples, diced
1/2 cup chopped nuts (omit for "no fat")

Topping:

1/2 teaspoon cinnamon
1/4 teaspoon nutmeg

1/4 cup sugar

BLEND FIRST 4 INGREDIENTS together in mixing bowl. Add next 5 ingredients and stir well. Fold in apples and nuts. Spread batter in greased 9 x 13-inch baking pan. Mix topping ingredients together and sprinkle over batter. Bake in a preheated 350 degree oven for 45 minutes. Cool in pan on wire rack. Serve warm or cold. Serves 8 to 12.

Dick & Ace Fields
MILL RACE FARM

Lemon Sponge Pie

Eleanor Hart of InnoScents Soap Company brings all-vegetable aromatherapy soaps to the Kittitas County Farmers' Market. She uses Kittitas County grown calendula, lavender, wild rose petals, and Douglas Fir in her soaps.

This is the most marvelous mouth-watering pie from an old Pennsylvania Dutch recipe from my family. Good winter or summer.

Unbaked pie shell
1 cup sugar
1 tablespoon flour
3 eggs, yolks and whites divided
1/3 cup lemon juice

1/4 teaspoon grated lemon rind
1/4 teaspoon salt
2 tablespoons melted butter
1 cup milk

BLEND SUGAR AND FLOUR together in large bowl. Add egg yolks, lemon juice, lemon rind, salt, and butter; mix well. Beat 3 egg whites until stiff, then fold into batter along with milk. Pour into unbaked pie shell and bake at 350 degrees for about 40 minutes or until lightly browned and firm. Serves 6.

Eleanor Hart
INNOSCENTS SOAP COMPANY

Flat Apple Pie

As American as apple pie, only baked on a cookie sheet.

2 1/2 cups flour
1/2 teaspoon salt
1 cup shortening
2 egg yolks
Water

5 to 7 apples, peeled and sliced
Butter
Sugar
Cinnamon

Glaze:
Powdered sugar
Lemon juice

MIX FLOUR, SALT, and shortening till crumbly. Beat egg yolks in a measuring cup, adding enough water to make 2/3 cup liquid. Add to dough and stir until combined. Roll dough on well-floured board to fit a cookie sheet, using 1/2 of the dough. Place on cookie sheet and cover bottom crust with apples. Dot with butter, sugar and cinnamon. Roll out remaining dough and place over apples for top crust. Make thin slits in top of crust so steam can escape.

Bake in a 375 degree oven for 50 minutes or until bubbly. After removing from oven, sprinkle with a glaze of powdered sugar and lemon juice. Serves 12.

Milly Bollinger
GREEN ACRE HOBBIES

---

the perfect pie crust

Work only with well-chilled ingredients.

• Pastry or all-purpose flour will produce a light, flaky crust. Whole wheat flour produces a heavier crust.

• Don't overwork dough. A light hand will produce a light crust.

• If you can't stand the heat, then neither can your pie dough. For better results, chill finished dough 1 hour before rolling out.

• Generously flour surface before rolling out dough.

• Work quickly so dough doesn't soften

• Roll from the center out, changing directions each time so dough rolls out in a circle.

• Lift and move dough every so often to make sure it's not sticking to surface.

Place aluminum foil or pie crust shield (available at kitchen stores) around the outer edge of the crust to prevent over browning.

Bleu Cheese Dressing · Great Grandma's Noodles

Queen Petri's Pesto · Salsa · Mock Guacamole

Smoked Fish Dip · Dill Pickles With A Spark

Kohlrabi Medley Soup · Clam Chowder

Curry Squash Soup · Baked Endive

Stewed Okra · Sicilian Pan Fry

Corn and Orange Pepper Delight · Zucchini Boats

Clam Fritters · Steamed Clams · Crab & Shrimp Cakes

Rhubarb Bread · Apple Cookies

Pineapple Bars · Blueberry Cobbler

Beet Chocolate Cake · Chocolate Zucchini Sheet Cake

Raw Apple Cake · Cream Cheese Frosting

Creamy Blender Chocolate Frosting · Carrot Cake

OLYMPIA FARMERS MARKET

LOCATION:
700 N. Capitol Way
April thru October
Thursday thru Sunday, 10:00 a.m. - 3:00 p.m.
November thru December
Saturdays & Sundays, 10:00 a.m. - 3:00 p.m.

The Olympia Farmers' Market features all locally grown foods and produced products, and is recognized as one of the largest and most successful markets in the country. With just 4 vendors selling in a livery stable at the turn of the century, the Market has now evolved into its current large covered structure with 80 stalls, 8 food vendors, a stage, and 1/3 acre of demonstration gardens showcasing native and wetland plants, herbs, bulbs, and a fabulous butterfly garden.

While shopping the Market you can enjoy spectacular waterfront views and the broad vista of the Olympic Mountain Range. And, you'll find just about anything from heirloom roses to specialty Asian produce to English cucumbers. You can travel the culinary world all while shopping at one market. Delicious Northwest products are also plentiful like herbal vinegars, jams and jellies, hazelnut products, plus fresh-caught fish including halibut, clams, and salmon.
Enjoy the family oriented live entertainment happening every week, and for Bluegrass music lovers there's a big Bluegrass Pickers Festival that goes on for 4 days during the third week in September. People from all over the country come just to enjoy the fantastic music. Other regular events include the big Chile and Barbecue cook-off happening during mid-August.

Bleu Cheese Dressing

Art comes in many forms—even wearable ones according to Carole Apple and Mary Kersten of Apple Creations. They have a lot of fun creating decorative sweatshirts, T-shirts, vests, and aprons for the Olympia Farmers' Market.

I got this from the Chart House in Hawaii. Great on a variety of salads, vegetables, and baked potatoes.

3/4 cup sour cream
1/2 teaspoon dry mustard
1/2 teaspoon black pepper
scant 1/2 teaspoon salt

1/4 teaspoon granulated garlic
1 teaspoon Worcestershire sauce
4 ounces imported Danish bleu cheese

BLEND ALL INGREDIENTS except bleu cheese in a bowl for 2 minutes at low speed, then 2 minutes more at medium speed. Crumble bleu cheese by hand into very small pieces; blend again at low speed for no longer than 4 minutes. Let set for 24 hours to allow the flavors to blend before using.

Mary Kersten
APPLE CREATIONS

Great Grandma's Noodles

Vicki Davis makes handmade Barbie doll clothes and accessories for her craft business, NaNa's Corner. Her specialty items are Barbie tents with matching sleeping bags. Look for her booth at the Olympia Farmers' Market.

Grandma was a Volga German immigrant. She came to America in 1878.

4 whole eggs
4 teaspoons water
Flour

MIX EGGS WITH WATER. Add flour to make a very stiff dough. Divide into 2 balls of dough. (Dust with extra flour if needed to keep dough from sticking to hands.) Roll out dough with a rolling pin; rolling thin enough so newsprint can be read. Place on wide flat surface to dry; allowing to dry to the quite dry but not brittle stage. Roll and slice into desired noodle widths with knife. Drop into boiling water or broth until cooked.

Vicki Davis
NANA'S CORNER

Queen Petri's Pesto

"Queenie" as Patrina Walker of Petri's is known, has been selling at the Olympia Farmers' Market since 1988. Her nickname came about due to the many crowns she sells. There are also postcards, stationery, notecards, doll clothes, mobiles and more. She even hand carves her own rubber stamp designs.

I've taught friends who aren't cooks to make this. It's easy, quick and delicious.

16 ounces olive oil
8 ounces pineapple or orange juice
3 to 4 bulbs (not cloves) of your favorite, garlic or one 8-ounce container of Tierra Bonita's Garlic & Cilantro Sauce

1 pound fresh basil (more to taste)
1 1/2 teaspoons salt
Grated Parmesan or Romano cheese
Roasted and chopped walnuts or pinenuts

IN A BLENDER, combine olive oil and juice. Add garlic and blend on high till thoroughly mixed. Gradually add basil and salt; blend again. The pesto should now be thick like pea soup. We bag up 3/4 cup pesto into each freezer bag, making 8 to 10 bags (freeze extras). When ready to use, cut tip end of bag and squeeze out onto any of the following: pasta, foccia, pizza, homemade bread, grilled chicken strips. Top with grated cheese and nuts if desired. Makes 8 to 10 bags.

Petrina L Walker
PETRI'S

Salsa

Shirley and Franklin Swenson of Swenson's Flower Patch sell more than just flowers. They also bring plants (including pond plants), bouquets, baskets, and holly wreaths to the Olympia Farmers' Market.

This salsa gets hotter as it ages.

10 to 12 large tomatoes, chopped
2 large onions, chopped
4 large bell peppers, chopped
2 4-ounce cans chopped green chiles
1/2 cup vinegar
1 6-ounce can tomato paste
1 tablespoon salt

1 1/2 teaspoons garlic powder
2 teaspoons chili powder
1 teaspoon chopped cilantro
1 teaspoon oregano
1/4 cup sugar
5 tablespoon cornstarch

PUT ALL INGREDIENTS in a large kettle. Bring to boil, reduce heat and simmer for 30 minutes. Pack into hot pint jars and seal. Refrigerate or process in boiling-water canner for 15 minutes. Yields approximately 6 pints.

Shirley L. Swenson
SWENSON'S FLOWER PATCH

Mock Guacamole

Sam and Marcia Flores of Hacienda Flores are selling their salsa products throughout the country, actually even in Saudi Arabia (it went with the troops), but they still call the Olympia Farmers' Market their home. They started with swap meets and various shows throughout the state, and now they even offer their products through their mail order catalog.

This is a delicious sauce that looks and taste like guacamole, minus the fat. The heat of sauce is regulated by the type of peppers used. Combine sweet and hot together for the best flavor. For a mild sauce, use sweet peppers only.

1 pound fresh peppers (mix sweet and
   hot for best flavor)
2 cloves garlic
1/2 teaspoon oregano
1/8 teaspoon black pepper

1 teaspoon salt, or to taste
1/2 fresh lime, juiced
6 cilantro stems with leaves
1/2 medium onion

ROAST OR CHAR peppers on grill, oven, or griddle. Place in a paper bag until cool. Remove skins and seeds. Mix all ingredients in blender and blend till smooth. It's ready!

Sam Flores
HACIENDA FLORES

container gardening

You don't need a huge yard to enjoy the beauty and benefits of growing flowers, fruits, vegetables, and herbs. Even when space is at a premium or limited to a patio balcony, you can still garden in containers. Just about anything can be grown in a container, even many trees. Soil, light, and nutrients are a few important factors for successful container gardening. Equally important are the type of container and plant variety you choose.

Plants grown in clay containers tend to dry out quicker and need watering more often than plants grown in plastic or ceramic pots. The amount of water a plant needs also depends on the size of container it's growing in. The larger the pot, the less often the plant needs water. Small or clay pots may need daily watering during the heat of summer, while a 24-inch or larger ceramic pot may only need to be watered 2 to 3 times a week. Plastic pots can eventually crack or weaken from exposure to the elements (sun, wind, cold). Wooden barrels might fall apart after 5 or more years of use. Large clay and ceramic pots can be difficult to move. Keep these things in mind when selecting your container.

Choose bush-type varieties when growing larger vegetables like melons, peppers, and tomatoes. A determinate tomato such as Oregon Spring, Bush Beefstake, Tiny Tim, or Patio will do better in a container than a vigorous indeterminate like Early Cascade. Grow cherry tomatoes in a hanging basket and allow the vines to cascade down the sides. Spacemaster Cucumber, Bambino Eggplant, Minnesota Midget Melon, Gold Rush Zucchini, and Burpee Butterbush Squash are also excellent candidates. For best production, use a minimum 5-gallon pot. Vegetables such as lettuce, carrots, onions, bush peas and beans, spinach, radishes, and even strawberries will do fine in containers having only 6 to 12-inches of soil, or grow several together in larger pots. A 24-inch container can hold up to 50 bush peas, 25 spinach plants, or 15 lettuce plants.

Use a good, well-drained potting mix (not native soil) and be sure your container has drainage holes in the bottom. Potting mix will not supply enough nutrients so you'll need to feed your plants with fish fertilizer, compost, manure tea or other complete organic fertilizer.

Save the sunless areas for shade loving herbs like parsley, mint, or chives. Tomatoes, peppers, eggplant, squash, beans, cucumbers, melons, and dwarf fruit trees really need ample light throughout the day to produce well. Other vegetables such as lettuce, peas, and spinach should do fine in part sun or under a covered patio.

Smoked Fish Dip

Next time you're at the Olympia Farmers' Market, look for Quirkworks. That's where you'll discover an assortment of hand-crafted polymer clay jewelry and other objects. It's no wonder that owners Linda Goff and Mr. Linda Goff (AKA Dan Kapsuer) list polymer clay slug items as their specialty. After all, they do live in the Northwest!

Although virtually any smoked fish can be used in this recipe, salmon or steelhead are preferred.

1/3 pound smoked fish, skin removed
8 ounces cream cheese
4 to 6 calamata olives, pitted and chopped
1 or 2 cloves garlic, minced

MIX INGREDIENTS together in food processor or blender until pureed. Serve on fresh raw vegetables, crackers, or dry toast for a delightful appetizer. Serves 6

Dan Kapsuer
QUIRKWORKS

---

garden quotes

"If you would have a mind at peace, a heart that cannot harden. Go find a door that opens wide upon a lovely garden."

Cypress Gardens

"What one approves, another scorns, and thus his nature each disclosed; You find the rosebush full of thorns, I find the thornbush full of roses."

Arthur Guiterman

"Why not go out on a limb? That's where the fruit is."

Will Rogers

"The greatest service which can be rendered any country is to add a useful plant to its culture."

Thomas Jefferson

"Work with your hands in the soil, it's the nearest thing to the all mighty above."

Martin B. Smith, grandfather to Martin J. Rose, market vendor

Dill Pickles With A Spark

Independence Valley Farm first began in 1982 selling at the Olympia Farmers' Market and to the wholesale market. Since then Betsie DeWreede has decided to focus on local marketing, so she started a CSA and continues to bring her organic produce to the farmers' market. Her specialties include pickling cucumbers, carrots, greens, strawberries, and popcorn.

This recipe may be doubled if you want to use 1/2 gallon jars. You can use medium or small cucumbers for 1/2 gallons.

10 pounds small pickling cucumbers
1 1/8 cups salt
6 1/2 cups cold water
7 cups cider vinegar
10 1/3 cups water
1 cup uniodized, pickling, or seasalt
6 1/2 tablespoons mustard

9 very large or 18 small cloves of garlic, peeled
18 heads of dill
2 Jalapeno peppers, chopped and divided into 9 piles (pepper and garlic may be omitted or increased to taste)

SOAK THE FIRST three ingredients in a large pot overnight. In a separate large pot, combine the vinegar, 10 1/3 cups water, salt, and mustard. Bring to a boil. Drain cukes that have been soaked overnight and place in hot quart jars. To each jar add 1 head of dill, 1 large (or 2 small) garlic cloves, and 1 pile of jalapenos. Fit these in bottom and middle spaces as you pack. Pour boiling liquid over cucumbers, leaving a 1/4-inch headspace. Seal and process in a boiling-water canner for 20 minutes. Let stand at least one month before using. Yields 9 quarts.

Betsie DeWreede
INDEPENDENCE VALLEY FARM

Kohlrabi Medley Soup

Located in the beautiful Skokomish Valley just 8 miles north of Shelton, Washington is Rose's Skokomish Valley Produce. Owners Martin and Coleen Rose sell off their farm and at the Olympia Farmers' Market, where all the splendor of their garden is displayed at their booth. Coleen also makes gift baskets, seasoning blends, potpourri, flower bouquets, Christmas wreaths, centerpieces, and arrangements.

Serve this delightful blend with hot rolls, bread sticks or crackers. Chicken, beef, pork, or meat of your choice can also be added, or serve as is with just vegetables.

6 cups chicken broth (vegetable or beef can also be used)
2 cups chicken (optional)
2 cups cubed kohlrabi
2 cups chopped onions
1 clove garlic, crushed
1 cup chopped spinach

2 cups chopped carrots
1 cup chopped celery
1 cup chopped parsnip
1 teaspoon basil (or 1 tablespoon chopped fresh basil)
Salt and pepper to taste

IN A LARGE KETTLE, combine all ingredients, cooking until meat is done and vegetables are tender. You may add more broth if needed. The soup may be thickened by ladling out 1 cup of vegetables and blending them in blender; pour back into soup and stir. A cornstarch thickening (mix 2 tablespoons cornstarch to 1/2 cup water) may also be added if you like a thicker soup. Serves 6.

Coleen F. Rose
ROSE'S SKOKOMISH VALLEY PRODUCE

beauty and the beast	What insect begins its life looking like a beastly miniature prehistoric alligator with tusk-like jaws, then evolves into a delicate beauty with slender body and transparent wings?
	Nicknamed "the aphid lion", a lacewing larvae can consume up to 60 aphids in just one hour and still be hungry enough to start all over again. With a voracious appetite, these creatures devour any soft-bodied insect and that includes whiteflies, mealybugs, spider mites, leafhopper nymphs, thrips, scales, caterpillar eggs, and of course, aphids. Sounds like a good friend to have around the garden! After feeding for up to three weeks, the larvae spin a shining cocoon where they make their transformation into the delicate-looking lacewing adult.
	Resembling a small dragonfly, the adult lacewing begins her 'search and destroy' mission where she can lay 400 to 600 eggs that will soon become the ferociously scary looking destroyers of pest insects everywhere.

Clam Chowder

Family owned and operated since the 1940's, Sound Fresh Clams & Oysters supplies the most diverse array of clams and oysters which are not available to the public elsewhere. All shellfish come fresh from the beach each morning. And you can also find their clams and oysters at the Olympia Farmers' Market. Their specialty is little Skookum Pacific Yearlings. Other unusual items include moon snails and eastern softshells.

This recipe comes from Amy Riggs who graduated from the Cordon Bleu School of Arts in London, England. Like spaghetti, the flavor of chowder improves with age.

8 to 10 pounds live clams (or 4 cups cooked, ground clams)
1/2 pound bacon, finely chopped
2 cloves garlic, minced
1 medium onion, finely chopped
1 stalk celery, peeled and finely chopped (keep covered in water until ready to use)
10 medium-sized potatoes, peeled and diced (keep covered in water until use)

Reserved clam nectar (1 to 2 pints)
Salt and pepper to taste
2 bay leaves
2 carrots, diced
1 12-ounce can of corn (or 2 cups grilled, fresh corn)
1 pint milk
1/4 cup butter (half stick), melted

STEAM THE CLAMS in a pot with 1 cup water (or a 1/2 can of beer) for seven to ten minutes, until the clams are open. Reserving the nectar, separate the meat from the shells; grind or finely chop the clam meat. Rinse the meat in a fine mesh colander to expel the softer bits.

Brown the bacon over medium heat, discarding all but 2 tablespoons of grease. Add onions, garlic, and celery to the bacon and sauté until translucent; then add chopped clams. Remove from heat and set aside.

Combine the reserved nectar (adding water to equal two pints of liquid if you are short on the nectar) and half of the diced potatoes in a large pot. Cook on medium heat until the potatoes are completely broken down, stirring frequently to prevent them from sticking and burning. Add corn, bay leaves, carrots, remaining potatoes, and the bacon and clam mixture to the pot. Simmer for 1 hour. Stir in milk and butter; season to taste with salt and pepper. Remove the bay leaves before serving. Serve with a fresh sourdough loaf or crusty French bread. Serves 10 to 12 as a main entree.

Amy Riggs
for SOUND FRESH CLAMS & OYSTERS

cooking with garlic

Roasted, baked, sautéed, or fresh; garlic can be cooked in many ways. The character of a dish can change depending on how garlic is prepared and when it is added. For a stronger garlic flavor, add fresh minced garlic to the dish after it is cooked. A milder flavor will develop if the garlic is cooked along with the dish, and for a really mellow flavor, try roasting or baking garlic first to bring out a nutty sweetness. When cooking garlic on the stove, be careful to not let it over brown or burn. The result can be bitter and the flavor may ruin the whole dish.

Curry Squash Soup

Use your favorite winter squash. If chanterelle or shiitake mushrooms aren't available, substitute regular 'button' mushrooms.

3 cups cooked mashed squash
2 1/2 cups water or stock
1 cup orange juice
2 tablespoons butter
1/2 cup chopped onion
1 clove garlic
1/2 teaspoon each cumin, coriander, and cinnamon

3/4 teaspoon ginger
1/4 teaspoon dry mustard
1 1/4 teaspoons salt
6 ounces mushrooms (chanterelle or shiitake)
Cayenne to taste
Lemon juice (optional)

BLEND SQUASH AND STOCK together in a large pot; add juice. Heat butter in a saucepan and sauté garlic, onion and spices until onion is translucent. Add mushrooms; cover and simmer 10 minutes. Add to soup pot and heat through. Season to taste with cayenne pepper and lemon (if too sweet).

Betsie DeWreede
INDEPENDENCE VALLEY FARM

Baked Endive

For over 10 years Michael Peroni of Flying Rhino has been catering to refined tastes with adventurous palates. He offers a wide variety of vegetables and specialty crops like gourmet greens and mushrooms through CSA delivery and the Olympia Farmers' Market.

Dive into a new experience of complex and complementary tastes.

1 tablespoon butter
1 tablespoon flour
1 cup milk
1 bunch endive

Salt and pepper to taste
2 ounces Gorgonzola cheese
3 tablespoons bread crumbs

MELT BUTTER in a saucepan over low heat and stir in flour till a thick paste forms. Slowly add milk to flour to make a simple white sauce. Bring to a slow boil, then lower to simmer. Stir occasionally while you carefully clean endive. Steam endive until just wilted.

Arrange endive in a shallow buttered baking dish; season to taste with salt and pepper. Spoon white sauce over endive. Break the cheese into small pieces over sauce; top with bread crumbs. Bake in a preheated 400 degree oven for about 10 minutes, or until lightly browned. Serves 2 to 4.

Michael Peroni
FLYING RHINO

Stewed Okra

Robert and Myrt Hawthorne sell a variety of bird feeders, bird houses, and crocheted items at the Olympia Farmers' Market.

A tasty combination of vegetables with mouth savoring flavor.

1 medium onion, diced
2 tablespoons oil
2 celery stalks, cut into bite-sized pieces
4 cloves garlic, minced
1 pound okra, stem end trimmed, cut into 1/2-inch pieces
1 teaspoon chopped fresh oregano (or 1/2 teaspoon dried)

1/2 teaspoon chopped fresh thyme (or 1/4 teaspoon dried)
1/4 teaspoon salt
1/4 teaspoon pepper
1/2 cup chicken broth
1-1/2 pounds plum tomatoes (about 6), peeled and cut into chunks

IN A SKILLET, heat oil over medium heat; add onion. Cook 2 minutes; stir occasionally. Add celery and garlic; cook and stir for 1 minute. Mix in okra and seasonings. Simmer about 5 minutes, then add broth and tomatoes. Cover and cook until okra is tender, about 5 minutes. Serves 4 to 6.

Myrt Hawthorne
HAWTHORNE'S CRAFTS

Sicilian Pan Fry

Serve this over pasta with grated Parmesan cheese. You can also substitute whatever vegetables are in season as desired.

10 to 12 stalks asparagus
Olive oil
1/2 medium onion, chopped
6 to 8 mushrooms, sliced
1 or 2 cloves garlic, diced

8 to 10 calamata olives, pitted and chopped
Dash of calamata brine, white pepper, oregano, and basil to taste

PREPARE ASPARAGUS into 1-inch sections of the tender stalk (snap off tough ends rather than cutting). Pour a bit of olive oil into frying pan and sauté onions for two minutes over medium heat. Add asparagus, mushrooms, garlic, and olives; stir to combine. Add seasonings to taste. Cover and cook till tender. Serves 2 to 3.

Dan Kapsuer
QUIRKWORKS

Corn and Orange Pepper Delight

A fresh, unique and tasty version of old-time creamed corn.

3 cups corn, cut off the cob (use
    frozen if fresh is not available)
1 cup chopped, mixed orange and
    green pepper
1 teaspoon sugar (optional)
1 cup water

2 tablespoons butter or margarine, melted
3/4 cup evaporated milk
2 tablespoons cornstarch
1/4 cup water
1 teaspoon each pepper and cumin
Johnny's seasoning (optional)

PUT CORN, PEPPERS, and sugar with 1 cup water in saucepan and cook vegetables until tender; remove from heat. Take out 1 1/2 cups cooked vegetables and put in blender along with melted butter and evaporated milk; blend until smooth. Pour mixture back into the saucepan, stirring constantly. Mix 1/4 cup water and cornstarch; while stirring, slowly add to vegetables until mixture starts to thicken. Add seasonings. Serves 5.

Coleen F. Rose
ROSE'S SKOKOMISH VALLEY PRODUCE

Zucchini Boats

Diamond Head Shave Ice and Chehalis Mints Company are two sweet places to see at the Olympia Farmers' Market. Selling at the market since she was 14, Jennifer Schofield knows how to cool summer down with refreshing tropical flavored shaved ice treats. Plus Mike and Sue Schofield bring plenty of milk chocolate mints, butter mints and more to the winter market.

Here's an all-American way to enjoy zucchini that will make you hope you never run out.

4 small-sized zucchini
2 pounds ground beef
1/4 cup mayonnaise
1 teaspoon lemon juice
2 teaspoons oregano

2 teaspoons parsley flakes
1 teaspoon onion salt
Pepper to taste
Spaghetti Sauce, your favorite
Grated cheddar cheese

CUT ZUCCHINI in half down the center. Scoop out the center flesh and reserve. In a medium bowl, mix together ground beef, mayonnaise, lemon juice, and seasonings. Add in flesh scoopings from zucchini. Put mixture in scooped out centers of zucchini. Use your favorite spaghetti sauce and pour over filling. Bake at 350 degrees for 30 to 40 minutes. Sprinkle with cheddar cheese the last few minutes. Serves 4.

Jennifer Schofield
DIAMOND HEAD SHAVE ICE

Clam Fritters

This recipe comes from Amy Riggs who graduated from the Cordon Bleu School of Culinary Arts in London, England. This is a true favorite.

24 large clams
1 microbrew beer-1/4 cup for cooking,
   the rest for enjoying
1 clove garlic, minced
2 eggs, lightly beaten

8 ounces (2/3 cup) corn
1 medium onion, finely chopped
Salt and pepper to taste
1 cup flour
3 to 4 tablespoons reserved bacon grease

STEAM THE CLAMS in a pot with 1/4 cup beer or water for 7 to 10 minutes, until the clams are open. (If clams are very fresh, no liquid is needed and the beer may be added for flavor only.) Grind or finely chop clam meat, and rinse in a fine mesh colander to expel the softer bits.

Combine garlic, eggs, corn, onion, and clam meat in a bowl; add salt and pepper to taste. Sprinkle flour on top and stir to blend. Batter should be pancake consistency and can be thinned, if necessary, with beer, clam nectar, or water. Spoon batter in a small amount of bacon grease and cook fritters until golden brown. Serve with lemon and butter.

Hint: Cook a few slices of bacon just before the fritters and reserve the grease for the recipe. Crumbled bacon makes a nice garnish for this dish. Serve with spicy cole slaw.

Amy Riggs
for SOUND FRESH CLAMS & OYSTERS

---

on the side

Steamed oysters are quick and easy. Here are some suggested seasonings and condiments to include next time you steam some up.

• A small dice of lime, red onion, tomato, and cilantro

• Sautéed bacon and onion

• Garlic lemon butter sauce

• Lemon juice

• Tabasco sauce

• Cocktail sauce

SOUND FRESH CLAMS & OYSTERS

Steamed Clams

This recipe comes from Amy Riggs who graduated from the Cordon Bleu School of Culinary Arts in London, England. For best results, choose a wide-bottom pot with a tight-fitting lid. Clams should not be more than two layers deep for even cooking.

3 pounds clams
1/2 cup liquid (water is fine, beer is better)
1 onion, sliced
1 to 1 1/2 tablespoons lemon juice
8 tablespoons unsalted butter

1/2 teaspoon dry mustard
1 teaspoon dried tarragon
Worcestershire sauce
Salt and pepper
1/2 lemon, sliced

RINSE CLAMS and place in a pot with a tight-fitting lid. Clams cook best if they are not more than two layers deep. Add 1/2 cup beer. Cover; bring to a boil on high heat, then reduce to medium. Steam 5 to 10 minutes until clams open. (Larger clams and native clams may take slightly longer.) Discard the unopened clams. While the clams are cooking, melt butter with dry mustard, lemon juice, tarragon, and a few drops of Worcestershire sauce. Season to taste with salt and pepper and garnish with lemon slices. Serves 2.

Amy Riggs
for SOUND FRESH CLAMS & OYSTERS

Crab & Shrimp Cakes

A new twist to an old favorite, Kitty Bell of Fossilwear sells tie dyed clothing at the Olympia Farmers' Market.

For a quick tarter sauce, mix 1/2 cup mayonnaise with 3 tablespoons dill pickle relish and a dash of Worcestershire sauce.

1 1/2 cups crabmeat
1 1/2 cups bay shrimp
2 eggs
1/3 cup flour

1/2 teaspoon salt
1 teaspoon minced garlic
2 green onions, finely chopped
2 tablespoons milk or cream

MIX ALL INGREDIENTS together in a bowl; crabmeat will break up as you mix. Overall texture will need to be moist, but not runny. If it is runny, add a bit more flour. Shape into individual small cakes and fry on an even temperature, preheated fry pan with a little butter or oil. Flip over after browned and semi-crisp on one side; cook other side. Serve hot with tarter sauce.

Kitty Bell
FOSSILWEAR

Rhubarb Bread

It's not hard to tell what Samira Kauthar and Karen Greene sell by the name of their business, Pottery In Motion; it's hand-crafted pottery of course.

You may have always thought of rhubarb and strawberries as the dynamic duo, but wait until you try rhubarb with applesauce.

1 tablespoon lemon juice
1 cup milk
1 1/2 cups brown sugar, packed
1/2 cup applesauce
1 egg

1 teaspoon baking soda
1 teaspoon vanilla extract
2 1/2 cups flour
2 cups diced fresh rhubarb

MIX LEMON JUICE and milk together and let sit for 10 to 15 minutes to sour. Beat brown sugar with applesauce and egg. Mix in vanilla. Add soda to soured milk. Add flour and soured milk alternately to brown sugar/applesauce mixture; blend well. Stir in rhubarb. Pour batter into two greased and floured 7 1/2 x 3 1/2-inch bread pans. Bake in preheated 325 degree oven for 1 hour or until toothpick inserted in middle comes out clean. Cool on wire racks. Makes 2 loaves.

Samira Kauthar
POTTERY IN MOTION

Apple Cookies

My grandma always makes apple cookies when the first apples ripen in summer. Make a powdered sugar frosting to spread over top.

1 egg, separated
Milk
2 1/2 cups sifted flour
1 tablespoon sugar
1 teaspoon salt

1 cup shortening
2/3 cup crushed corn flakes
5 cups sliced apples
1 1/2 cups sugar
1 teaspoon cinnamon

PUT EGG YOLK in a measuring cup and add enough milk to equal 2/3 cup. Mix flour, sugar, and salt together in separate bowl. Cut in shortening. Roll out half of dough to a 15 x 11-inch rectangle. Place on cookie sheet. Cover with crushed corn flakes, then arrange apples on top. Sprinkle sugar and cinnamon over apples.

Roll out other half of dough and put it over apples; sealing up the edges. Beat egg white till stiff; spread over top crust with a pastry brush. Bake in a preheated 375 degree oven for 40 minutes.

Jennifer Schofield
DIAMOND HEAD SHAVE ICE

Pineapple Bars

Try a little variation for the frosting and add any of the following: grated orange rind, shredded coconut, or dash of vanilla.

1/2 cup butter	2 cups flour
1 cup brown sugar	1 teaspoon baking powder
1 egg	1 teaspoon baking soda
1 small can crushed pineapple with juice	

COMBINE ABOVE in a bowl. Pour batter into a 9 x 13-inch pan and bake at 350 degrees for 20 minutes or until done. Frost with the following:

6 tablespoons browned butter	Chopped nuts or crushed granola
1 1/2 cups powdered sugar	

Mix butter and sugar with enough hot water so that it spreads easily. Frost pineapple bars, then sprinkle with chopped nuts or crushed granola.

Mary Kersten
APPLE CREATIONS

the name says it all	What popular beverage originally included a combination of wintergreen, hops, juniper, spikenard, and a dozen other roots and berries?
	First advertised nationally in 1893 as a bottled drink, a Philadelphia druggist named Hires first launched his creation at the Philadelphia Exposition in 1876 under the name of "Root Beer".

Blueberry Cobbler

You'll find 100% pure essential oils with no animal products in Falls Creek Soapworks' all natural vegetable soaps. Gretchen Stangl-Charlton and Wendy Stern, "self-taught" soapmakers, also bring hand-woven baskets, handmade paper boxes and bags to the Olympia Farmers' Market.

I created this recipe from a combination of two others and I really like it because it worked out so well and it really tastes great.

    2 pints fresh blueberries (24 ounces
        if using frozen)
    2 teaspoons cornstarch
    1/2 to 2/3 cup sugar

WASH BLUEBERRIES, drain well and put into small mixing bowl. Combine cornstarch and sugar; sprinkle over blueberries and stir well. Pour into 8-inch square glass baking dish.

    3 tablespoons sugar   1 1/2 cups unbleached flour
    1 tablespoon baking powder   1/4 cup chilled butter, cut into small cubes
    1/4 teaspoon baking soda   1 cup buttermilk
    1/4 teaspoon salt

COMBINE IN A MEDIUM BOWL all dry ingredients; mix well. Using fingertips or pastry blender, run in butter until mixture resembles coarse cornmeal. Add buttermilk and stir until moist clumps form. Spoon batter over blueberries. Bake in a preheated 375 degree oven for 35 minutes or until juices bubble and top is golden brown. Serve warm or at room temperature. Makes 6 servings.

Gretchen Stangl-Charlton
FALLS CREEK SOAPWORKS

Beet Chocolate Cake

Are you in for a surprisingly awesome taste. Sprinkle powdered sugar on top or frost with frosting of your choice, and you have a winner.

1 cup oil
1 1/2 cups sugar
3 eggs
1 3/4 cups flour
1 1/2 teaspoons baking soda

1 teaspoon salt
1 1/2 cups cooked pureed beets
1 teaspoon vanilla
2 ounces melted chocolate*

** Or substitute 1 1/4 cups semi-sweet cocoa, or 1/4 cup carob powder plus 2 teaspoons vanilla
and 1 teaspoon cinnamon*

IN A LARGE BOWL, cream together the oil, sugar and eggs. Add dry ingredients; stir to combine. Mix in beets, vanilla and chocolate. Pour batter into a greased 9 x 13-inch pan or bunt pan and bake at 350 degrees for 25 to 30 minutes or until toothpick inserted in the middle comes out clean. Top with favorite frosting. Serves 10 to 15.

Coleen F. Rose
ROSE'S SKOKOMISH VALLEY PRODUCE

---

berry basics

Blackberries grace much of the Northwest and can be trailing, upright or even thornless. Availability depends on location but can begin in June and continue through September. Different varieties will produce a difference in taste. Use for pies, jams, jellies and fresh eating.

Blueberries are a long-lived bush that gives a very striking effect in the landscape. Great for fresh eating, pies and jams. Available July through September, sometimes October.

Boysenberries are a type of blackberry. The fruit is large, reddish-black with a delightful hint of raspberry flavor. Great fresh, frozen, in pies or preserves.

Cranberries are cousins to the lingonberry and blueberry. A familiar sight at Thanksgiving, these shiny red berries ripen in September or October.

Gooseberries are famous in pies, jams, jellies, pudding or as a sauce. Translucent striped fruit can be green, pink or red. Berries are large, round and high in Vitamin C.

Huckleberries are a shrub native to the Northwest. Related to blueberries, the fruit is slightly smaller and makes delicious pies, jams, jellies or syrups.

Jostaberries have a flavor that grows on you when eaten fresh and also makes terrific jam. The taste is reminiscent of grape and kiwi, and the fruit ripens during June and July. The purple-black berry is a cross between a black currant and a gooseberry.

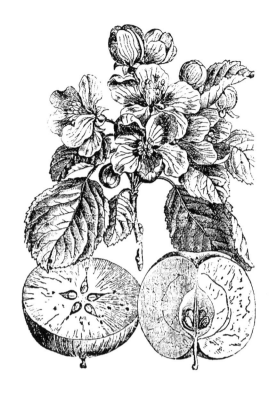

more berry basics	Lingonberry is an evergreen ground cover with tart red berries that are used for preserves, syrups and wine.

Loganberries have a unique and highly-prized flavor. Thought to be a cross between a blackberry and a red raspberry, the large, elongated maroon fruit is eaten fresh, canned, and used in pies and for wine.

Marionberry, a type of blackberry, has an excellent but sweet wild berry flavor and is delicious fresh, or for use in canning, freezing, pies, jam and wine. Ripens slightly before other blackberries.

Raspberries begin ripening in June, with the everbearing type producing into fall. Mostly red, there are also gold and black varieties. The texture is somewhat dry with a perfumed aroma.

Salmonberries are plentiful in the Pacific Northwest forests and the first berries to ripen. Related to raspberries, the flavor of the golden berry is less pronounced.

Strawberries are in high demand and it's easy to understand why. Thank goodness this bright red berry is ready in early June, and by planting different varieties, berries production can continue through September.

Tayberry is a cross between a loganberry and a black raspberry. The large reddish-black berry is very long on size and flavor.

Chocolate Zucchini Sheet Cake

Once a dairy farm, Alice and Ray Parker of Parker's Produce now raise hay and lots of juicy sweet corn for the Olympia Farmers' Market.

Now when you say the word "zucchini" it will bring a sweet smile to anyone's face.

2 cups sugar
1 cup oil
3 eggs
2 1/2 cups flour
1/4 cup baking cocoa
1 teaspoon baking soda

1/4 teaspoon baking powder
1/4 teaspoon salt
1/2 cup milk
2 cups shredded fresh zucchini
1 tablespoon vanilla extract

IN A LARGE MIXING bowl, combine sugar and oil. Add eggs one at a time, beating well after each addition. Combine flour, cocoa, baking soda, baking powder, and salt. Gradually add to the egg mixture alternating with the milk. Stir in the zucchini and vanilla. Pour into a greased 15 x 10 x 1-inch baking pan. Bake at 375 degrees for 25 minutes or until cake is done. While cake is baking, make frosting (recipe follows). Spread frosting over cake while hot. Cool on wire rack. Serves 10 to 15.

Frosting

1/2 cup butter or margarine
6 tablespoons evaporated milk
1 tablespoon vanilla extract

1/4 cup baking cocoa
1 pound (4 cups) confectioners sugar

Cream butter, milk, and vanilla together in a medium bowl. Add presifted cocoa and confectioners sugar; mix until smooth.

Alice Parker
PARKER'S PRODUCE

---

pick a peck of sweet peppers

Sweet peppers come in a variety of different shapes and vivid colors. A green pepper is a sweet pepper that just hasn't fully matured and ripened to its final color.

Most all sweet peppers begin growing as a green pepper although there are a few varieties where the pepper will start growing its fruit in colors like purple, pale yellow or greenish-yellow.

A pepper will be its sweetest after it has fully developed and turned its final color, and that can be shades of red, gold, yellow, orange or even chocolate depending on the variety.

Raw Apple Cake

Deliciously moist and tender. Top with cream cheese frosting or creamy blender chocolate frosting. (Recipes follow.)

3 cups flour
1/2 teaspoon salt
1 teaspoon baking soda
1 teaspoon nutmeg
1 teaspoon cinnamon
2 cups sugar

3 cups chopped apples
1 1/2 cups chopped nuts
3 eggs, slightly beaten
1 1/2 cups canola oil
2 teaspoon vanilla

SIFT DRY INGREDIENTS together in a large bowl. Stir in apples and nuts. In a small bowl, combine eggs, oil, and vanilla, mix well then add to dry ingredients; stir to combine. Pour batter into a greased tube pan or 9 x 13-inch dish. Bake in a 350 degree oven for 1 hour or until knife inserted in the middle comes out clean. Allow to cool before frosting. Serves12 to 15.

Mary Kersten
APPLE CREATIONS

Cream Cheese Frosting

Good as a topping on cakes, cupcakes, and cookies.

1/2 cup margarine, melted
1 8-ounce package cream cheese, softened

1 teaspoon vanilla
1 pound box powdered sugar

COMBINE MARGARINE, cream cheese, and vanilla in medium bowl. Gradually add powdered sugar and beat until smooth.

Mary Kersten
APPLE CREATIONS

Creamy Blender Chocolate Frosting

This frosting is absolutely scrumptious!

6 ounces (blocks) unsweetened
  baking chocolate
1 1/2 cups sugar

1 cup evaporated milk
1 teaspoon vanilla
6 tablespoons margarine

CUT CHOCOLATE INTO smaller pieces, then put all ingredients in a blender. Cover and blend at low speed until larger pieces of chocolate are chopped. Stop motor and stir. Blend at high speed until frosting becomes thick and creamy. Makes about 3 cups.

Mary Kersten
APPLE CREATIONS

cooking tip	If you want to add flavor to foods without adding a lot of salt, try soy sauce instead. Teaspoon for teaspoon, soy sauce has less sodium than salt (460mg versus a whopping 2,300 mg).

Carrot Cake

This cake is so moist and delicious, it's a sure hit with anyone.

2 cups sugar
1 1/2 cups oil
1 teaspoon vanilla
4 eggs
3 cups grated carrots

2 cups flour
2 teaspoons baking powder
1/2 teaspoon salt
2 teaspoons baking soda
2 teaspoons cinnamon

CREAM TOGETHER the sugar, oil and vanilla. Add eggs, one at a time, beating after each addition. Mix in carrots. Sift together in a separate bowl, flower, baking soda and powder, salt, and cinnamon. Add to wet ingredients and mix well. Pour batter into a greased and floured 9 x 13-inch pan. Bake at 375 degrees for 1 hour. Allow cake to cool, then top with cream cheese frosting. Serves 12 to 15.

Shirley L. Swenson
SWENSON'S FLOWER PATCH

Pike Market Senior Center's Festive Salsa

Raspberry Rose Petal Dip · Zucchini Ghannouj

Croissants Stuffed with Shiitake and Herb Duxelles

Sizzling Marinade

Oyster Mushroom and Roasted Hazelnut Stuffing

Nutty Nutri Salad · All-American Potato Salad

Sugar Snap Pea Sauté · Stir-Fried Harvest Medley

Hash Browns

Sweet and Sour Oyster Mushrooms with Vegetables

Low Fat Veggie Burritos · Stuffed Melenzana

Garbanzo-Meatball Stew · Chicken and Oyster Mushrooms

Zucchini Bread · Thumbprint Cookies

Chocolate Covered Cherries · Raspberry Shortcakes

Yummy Apple Sage Pie · Chrisman Farms Rolled Cake

PIKE PLACE MARKET

LOCATION:
1st & Pike Street in Downtown Seattle
Year Round
Open 7 days a week
8:00 a.m. - 5:00 p.m. winter hours
8:00 a.m. - 6:00p.m. through fall

THE PIKE PLACE MARKET ORIGINALLY TOOK ROOTS BACK IN 1907 AND HAS NOW BECOME known to many as "The Heart and Soul of Seattle". A public market owned by the people of Seattle and managed by a non-profit social service agency known as the Pike Place Market Preservation & Development Authority, it is one of the nation's oldest continuously operating public markets. One of Seattle's most popular tourist destinations attracting more than 9 million visitors a year, it is the first National Historic District created by a vote of the people.

Pike Place is also a working farmers' market with more than 100 farmers selling fresh produce, fruits and flowers year round. There are also about 45 non-restaurant food merchants in the Market, representing nearly every kind of fish, meat, produce and specialty food imaginable.

In addition to the food that shoppers take home with them, more than four dozen restaurants, cafes and food bars reside within the Market Historical District. Plus there's plenty of specialty crafts, clothing and gifts to brighten someone's life, perhaps even your own.

Pike Market Senior Center's Festive Salsa

The Pike Market Senior Center provides social services to area seniors. Other services include an employment program, referral service, social worker services, group activities, and free meals.

It's amazing how just a few ingredients can add up to tremendous flavor.

12 roma tomatoes
4 Walla Walla sweet onions
2 bunches cilantro

3 to 15 Jalapeno peppers,
   strictly to taste (remove seeds)
6 limes

WASH AND CHOP tomatoes, onions, cilantro, and peppers. Toss with juice of limes. Enjoy with your favorite chips or vegetable.

PIKE MARKET SENIOR CENTER

Raspberry Rose Petal Dip

If you want fantastic flavor in your herbal jams, vinegars, and jellies, then go see Rachel-Dee Herb Farm at the Pike Place Market. Ivonne Brown and her husband Eugene grow their own organic fruits and herbs for their products. Customer favorites are the Raspberry Mint Jam and Garlic Jelly.

Banana chunks, fresh strawberries, grapes, and slices of pear or apples are deliciously enhanced by this dip. Try different herbal jellies for a change in flavors like Sweet Basil or Purple Ruffles.

4 ounces cream cheese
1/2 jar Raspberry Rose Petal Jelly*
Assorted fresh fruit

* Available through Rachel-Dee Herb Farm at the Pike Place Market.

SOFTEN CREAM CHEESE in microwave for 20 seconds or until it becomes workable. Add herbal jelly. Using a fork or whisk, continue beating together until mixture becomes smooth. Pour into small serving dish and surround with wedges and slices of fresh fruit. If dip becomes too firm for dipping, add 1/2 teaspoon of milk to mixture, beating until smooth.

Ivonne Brown
RACHEL-DEE HERB FARM

Zucchini Ghannouj

Mark Musick has been involved with the growing and marketing of food in the Northwest for the last 25 years. One of the original founders of Tilth, he now serves as Farmer Coordinator for the Pike Place Market. Both Mark and wife Terry Mendenhall are part of an agricultural co-housing community on Vashon Island in Puget Sound.

This is a unique version of a classic Middle Eastern dip, using over-grown "bomber zucchini" rather than eggplant. It's the ultimate answer for what to do with "the ones that get away".

1 very large zucchini	1/4 cup sesame butter or olive oil
4 to 5 cloves garlic	3 teaspoons cumin
1/3 cup lemon juice	1 teaspoon chipotle pepper (powdered)

PREHEAT OVEN TO 350 DEGREES. Slice open zucchini lengthwise, remove the seeds and roast about 45 minutes or until most of the moisture is evaporated from the flesh. When the zucchini pulp is dry, remove from oven and allow to cool. Scrape out flesh and place in a food processor. Add remaining ingredients and process until the texture is smooth and creamy.

The chipotle pepper gives Zucchini Ghannouj the warm, smoky flavor of the traditional eggplant version. Serve as a dip with crackers or veggie sticks. Zucchini Ghannouj can be served fresh, or it freezes well for year-round enjoyment.

Terry Mendenhall and Mark Musick
PIKE PLACE MARKET

---

time saving kitchen tips

Crush whole nuts with ease. Just put desired amount inside a plastic bag and crush with a rolling pin.

Measure and snip fresh herbs all in the same measuring cup with a pair of scissors

Tie up a bundle of fresh herbs like rosemary, thyme, oregano, or basil. Dip herb bundle in marinade when barbecuing and brush right on the meat or vegetables. Right before the barbecue is ready, toss the herb bundle right on the coals for sealed-in smoked herb flavor.

A salad spinner works wonders at removing excess water from salad greens. Greens run through a salad spinner keep twice as long in the crisper drawer of the refrigerator as unspun greens.

Have extra tomatoes but not enough to make into salsa or sauce? Just pop ripe whole tomatoes in a snap and seal type freezer bag and toss in the freezer. Then when it's time to peel the skin, hold frozen fruit under hot tap water—skins slip right off.

When dinner gets started late but appetites are ready now, reduce cooking time by cutting foods into smaller pieces before you cook.

For hot pasta in a snap, start with hot tap water, not cold. And be sure to add some salt to the cooking water. Salted water boils faster than unsalted, and hot water boils faster than cold.

Croissants Stuffed with Shiitake and Herb Duxelles

Bob and Harriet Ames of Skunk Bay Mushrooms began their farm back in 1991. They grow certified organic mushrooms like oyster, shiitake, lion's mane, maitake, and enoki using locally grown straw and alder. You can find their unusual and medicinal mushrooms at Pike Place Market, Sequim and Bainbridge Island Farmers' Markets.

The duxelles is a thick paste or sauce with noticeable pieces of mushroom and onion. It can be prepared in advance and stored in the freezer for later use. Croissants should be made in advance or purchased fresh from a bakery.

3 tablespoons melted butter	1/4 teaspoon salt
2/3 cup chopped onions	1/4 teaspoon sugar
2 cups chopped shiitake mushrooms	1/2 teaspoon soy sauce
1/2 teaspoon Italian seasoning	

SAUTÉ ONIONS IN BUTTER until they become transparent. Add the remaining ingredients and cook until the liquid has evaporated and a paste-like mixture is formed. Slice croissants in half and fill with duxelles. Place these on a baking sheet and warm in the oven at 350 degrees for 3 to 5 minutes. Serve with soup or salad. Makes 4 to 6 servings.

Bob & Harriet Ames
SKUNK BAY MUSHROOMS

---

cooking with specialty mushrooms

Specialty mushrooms are very different from the white button mushrooms in flavor, shape, and texture. Generally speaking, these mushrooms are not eaten raw because cooking enhances their digestibility and flavor. One exception, however, is the enoki mushroom which is wonderful in salads or used as a fresh garnish.

Shiitake mushrooms are native to Asia and have a good earthy flavor and meaty texture. They lend themselves to any recipe that calls for mushrooms, especially spicy pasta sauces. We use them in vegetable stir-frys, in meat dishes, or as a meat substitute.

Maitake's toasted almond-like flavor has put this mushroom at the top of the list as our favorite. The maitake mushroom is getting considerable attention by researchers for its ability to stimulate the immune system. Break into bite-size pieces and slice the remainder in 1/8-inch thick slices. Sauté in olive oil to develop the wonderful toasted almond flavor. Very good with sautéed snow peas.

Lion's Mane is a mild mushroom with flavor and texture similar to crab. Native to North America, they are produced by only a very few commercial mushroom growers. Slice in 1/4 to 1/2-inch thick slices and sauté until a light golden color. Best enjoyed sautéed with a little garlic and butter, or with foods such as eggs, seafood, or poultry. Try sautéed sliced mushrooms covered with warmed goat cheese and herbs.

Oyster mushrooms have an excellent texture with a nice nutty flavor. Native to the Pacific Northwest, this is one of the first specialty mushrooms to be cultured commercially in this country. Very good in omelets, vegetable or meat stir-fry, or even on a pizza. Cut in 1-inch size pieces. The stem is edible and should be sliced thin.

Enoki mushrooms can vary in shape, size and color, depending on the culture conditions. We prefer to grow it under more natural conditions to develop the beautiful color and rich flavor. Both the cap and stems are edible. Enoki is very good raw in a salad or used as a garnish. It can also be sautéed lightly and added to your favorite rice or pasta dish.

Bob & Harriet Ames, Skunk Bay Mushrooms

Sizzling Marinade

Kevin Roy of Sotto Voce has been bringing his fine line of flavored oils and vinegars to the Pike Place Market since 1992. Using a traditional infusion method, they produce small batches of 100% natural premium quality spiced and herbed olive oils and vinegars.

Fresh basil, soy sauce, and herbal vinegar go perfect with steak, stir-fry, hamburgers, or a spicy salad.

1/4 cup soy sauce
1/4 cup chopped onion
2 cloves crushed garlic

1 tablespoon chopped fresh basil
1/2 cup Aceto Tre Colori*
　(specialty herbal vinegar)

* *Available through Sotto Voce by mail order or at the Pike Place Market.*

MIX ALL INGREDIENTS and pour over meat. Marinate in refrigerator for 4 hours. Cook, serve, and enjoy.

Kevin Roy
SOTTO VOCE

coriander versus cilantro	Even though it comes from the same plant (Coriandrum sativum), coriander and cilantro are used quite differently. The lacy green leaves of coriander are known as cilantro, while the spherically-shaped seed from the mature plant results in the spice, coriander. Some books reference the flavor of cilantro as that of a combination of sage and citrus, while coriander has more of a citrus taste.
	There's a long history of use for coriander beginning with the Bible, when in the Sinai wilderness the starving Hebrews were fed manna from Heaven and said, "it was like white coriander seed", Exodus 16:31. And when the colonists arrived to America, it was one of the first herbs they grew.
	Coriander spice has a warm, sweet and aromatic flavor that is commonly used in curries, spice mixtures, baked goods, pastries and candies. Store the seed in airtight jars where the flavor will improve with age.
	Also known as Chinese parsley, cilantro's pungent leaves take a prominent place in many Mediterranean, Chinese, Thai, Cambodian and Mexican dishes. The young leaves are said to have a grassy and citrusy sage-like flavor. The herb is best used fresh. Of cilantro it is said that you either love the herb or you hate it. Now I love the flavor of citrus and sage, but I can't taste either in cilantro.

Oyster Mushroom and Roasted Hazelnut Stuffing

The Holmquist family is a large grower of hazelnuts, and they bring them roasted, toasted, salted, in quick breads and cookies—any way you like 'em. Even plain in the shell. Speaking of shells, Holmquist Hazelnut Orchards has plenty and sells them bulk at the Pike Place Market and University District Farmers' Market. They make great mulch!

Roasted hazelnuts, oyster mushrooms, and the fresh herb flavor of rosemary and sage blend to wonderful perfection.

1 1/2 loaves of bread, cut into
   half-inch cubes
1 pound hazelnuts, roasted and
   coarsely chopped
1 stick butter (1/2 cup)
3 medium onions, chopped
1 pound oyster mushrooms, sliced
   (can also use shiitake)

5 celery stalks, chopped
1/2 pound prosciutto or other
   thin-sliced ham (optional)
4 tablespoons chopped fresh rosemary
3 tablespoons chopped fresh sage
Chicken stock

DRY BREAD IN ADVANCE, spread out on sheet pans and bake at 350 degrees for 20 minutes; stir occasionally. Roast hazelnuts on a baking sheet at 350 degrees for 12 minutes. Melt butter in large sauté pan over medium-high heat. Add onions and cook until golden brown. Add mushrooms and cook until they begin to release their juices; about 5 minutes. Add celery and cook a few minutes more. Remove from heat. Stir in prosciutto and mix with dry bread. Add fresh herbs and moisten with chicken stock, Use as you would any dressing or stuffing. Makes about 16 cups dressing.

The Holmquist Family
HOLMQUIST HAZELNUT ORCHARDS

---

how hot is hot?

The heat of a pepper can vary immensely all the way from the mild Anaheim to the fiery hot Habanero. Measured in units of heat, the Scoville pepper scale registers the mild Anaheim at 1,000 to 1,500 units, medium hot Jalapeno at 35,000 to 45,000 units, and flaming Habanero, thought to be the hottest pepper, at 200,000 to 300,000 units. The following peppers are listed in order of heat, with the hottest pepper being first.

1. Habanero
2. Scotch Bonnet
3. Thai Paper Dragon
4. Super Chili
5. Tabasco
6. Fire
7. Mushroom
8. Cayenne Long Red Slim
9. Cherry Bomb
10. Serrano Chili
11. Garden Salsa
12. Early Jalapeno
13. Hot Banana
14. Ancho
15. Tam Jalapeno
16. Mulato Isleno
17. Anaheim Chili
18. Passilla Bajio

Nutty Nutri Salad

Susan Wells and Eric Alexander's business has really sprouted in a big way, literally. They grow sprouts—lots and lots. There's sunflower and buckwheat, popular veggies like broccoli, radish, and pea, plus spicy favorites like mustard, cress, and arugula sprouts. Fresh and natural, healthy and wholesome sprouts from Sunflower Farms. Look for them at the Pick Place Market and University District Farmers' Market.

Yes, sunflower greens are better than edible, they're delicious! Add to that the nutty rich flavors of almonds and beans accented by the sweetness of raisins and you've got an instant classic.

1 cup sunflower greens
1 cup buckwheat lettuce
1/4 cup garbanzo beans, soaked 12 hours
1/4 cup lentils, soaked 12 hours

1/4 cup raw sunflower seeds
1/4 cup raisins
8 or 10 raw almonds, soaked 12 hours
Chopped onion to taste

RINSE SOAKED BEANS, lentils, and almonds. Mix sunflower greens and buckwheat lettuce together in serving bowl. Sprinkle all other ingredients on top of greens, then sprinkle to taste with rice vinegar. Serves 4.

Susan Wells
SUNFLOWER FARMS

All-American Potato Salad

Jan and Peter Alden turned a dairy farm into a gourmet fare—they grow acres and acres of organically-grown specialty potatoes, 15 different varieties. Organic vegetables are also grown at Alden Farms. Look for them on Wednesdays at Pike Place Market, Thursdays at Snohomish Farmers' Market, and Saturdays at the University District Farmers' Market.

A colorful medley of specialty potatoes makes this a very special salad.

1 pound All Blue potatoes
1 pound Yukon Gold potatoes
1 pound Red Gold potatoes
3 hard-boiled eggs
1 cup diced celery
3/4 cup diced green pepper
1/2 cup diced red onion
1/2 cup finely chopped fresh parsley

1 cup Simple Mayonnaise (recipe follows)
1/4 cup plain yogurt
1 tablespoon mustard (or to taste)
2 tablespoons cider vinegar
2 teaspoons sugar
Salt and freshly ground black pepper
Paprika for sprinkling

IN A LARGE POT, cover potatoes with water. Bring to a boil and cook over medium heat for 35 to 40 minutes, or until tender. Drain the potatoes and let them cool slightly. Quarter the potatoes lengthwise (go ahead, leave the skins on), then cut into 1/2-inch thick slices. Put potatoes in a large bowl along with eggs, celery, green pepper, onion, and parsley; toss to combine.

In a small bowl, whisk together the mayonnaise, yogurt, mustard, vinegar, and sugar. Gently mix the dressing into the potatoes while still warm. Season with salt and pepper, then sprinkle with paprika. Serves 6 to 8.

Simple Mayonnaise:

1 whole egg
1 egg yolk
3 tablespoons fresh lemon juice

3/4 cup plus 2 tablespoons
    vegetable oil
2 tablespoons olive oil

Combine whole egg and egg yolk along with lemon juice in blender or food processor. Blend 20 to 30 seconds. With machine still running, pour in vegetable oil and olive oil in a very slow, steady stream and blend until mixture is thick. Store in the refrigerator for up to 3 days.

Jan Alden
ALDEN FARMS

Sugar Snap Pea Sauté

Seattle area restaurants were the first to serve Willie Green's Organic Farm's delicious organic greens. Now Jeff Miller and Heidi Blackburn are selling directly to consumers through a CSA program and at the Pike Place Market and University District Farmers' Market. Sample some of their delicious fruits, vegetables, and of course salad mixes for yourself.

Sugar snap peas are the epitome of spring—sweet like the blooming flower, crisp like the fresh air, and full of lively flavor.

1 pound sugar snap peas	2 tablespoons chicken stock
2 tablespoons butter	Salt and pepper to taste

REMOVE THE STRINGS from both sides of pods. Bring a large pan of salted water to a boil. Add the pea pods and blanch for 2 minutes. Drain and rinse with cold water until the pods are cold as well.

When ready to serve, melt 1 tablespoon butter in a skillet over medium heat. Add the pea pods and sauté 1 to 2 minutes, being careful not to brown the butter. Add stock and bring to a quick boil. Remove from heat and stir in remaining tablespoon butter. Season with salt and pepper, then serve. Makes 4 servings.

Heidi Blackburn
WILLIE GREEN'S ORGANIC FARM

In a pinch

What to do when the recipe calls for honey but all you have is sugar and you don't know how much to use? Here's a list of some replacements that will do in a pinch along with the suggested amounts to use.

For	Use
1 tablespoon flour	1/2 tablespoon cornstarch
1 tablespoon cornstarch	2 tablespoon flour
1 cup cake flour	7/8 cup all-purpose flour
1 1/2 teaspoons cornstarch	1 tablespoon flour
1 teaspoon baking powder	1/4 teaspoon baking soda plus 1/2 teaspoon cream of tartar
1 1/2 cups corn syrup	1 cup sugar plus 1/2 cup water
1 cup honey	1 to 1 1/4 cups sugar plus 1/4 cup liquid
1 cup sugar	1/2 to 1 cup honey less 1/4 cup liquid
1 cup sour milk	1 cup milk plus 1 tablespoon vinegar or lemon juice
1 cup milk	1 cup sour milk or buttermilk plus 1/2 teaspoon baking soda
1 cup milk	1/2 cup of evaporated milk plus 1/2 cup water
1 cup crumbs	23 soda crackers, crushed; or 15 graham crackers, crushed
1 ounce unsweetened chocolate	3 tablespoons cocoa plus 1 tablespoon fat

Stir-Fried Harvest Medley

Judy and Dave Duff of Duffield Farms have become a real favorite for chefs and home cooks who shop at the Pike Place Market. They sell a wide variety of fresh vegetables including specialty greens and herbs.

The subtle hint of mustard flavor delightfully mingles with sesame and peppery nasturtiums to compliment a variety of tasty garden produce.

1 tablespoon canola oil
1/2 cup chopped onion
3/4 cup broccoli florets
4 small summer squash, cut into
   1/2 x 1-inch pieces
1 cup Hericot vert green beans, cut into
   1-inch pieces (French/filet type)
1 cup chopped Mizuna greens
   (type of Oriental green)

1/2 cup chopped Shungiku
   (edible chrysanthemum)
1 cup Tat Soy or baby Bok Choy with
   whole leaves (tat soy, tatsoi,
   tah tsai; all the same)

1/4 cup sesame seeds, toasted
8 fresh edible nasturtium flowers

IN A LARGE SKILLET OR WOK, heat oil over medium-high heat until very hot. Add onion and stir-fry for 2 minutes. Add in vegetables and greens and stir-fry to desired doneness, about 3 to 5 minutes. Add 1 or 2 tablespoons of water while stir-frying if you like your vegetables cooked to a more tender stage. Place on dinner plates, then sprinkle with sesame seeds and arrange nasturtiums on top immediately before serving. Serves 4.

Judy & Dave Duff
DUFFIELD FARMS

Hash Browns

Jerry Goronea and Anne Read began River Farm in 1977. They use sustainable and soil-building techniques that imitate nature. Their biggest reward, seeing an organic system come alive, has also been their biggest challenge economically—in managing an organic approach. They sell at Pike Place Market, Kittitas County and University District Farmers' Markets.

This delicious dish should be served at breakfast, lunch, and dinner. For a flavorful variation, sprinkle grated garlic or powdered dried peppers over top.

1 1/2 pounds potatoes (russets or thin skinned variety)	1/2 cup grated cheese, such as Cheddar, Mozzarella, or Romano
2 tablespoons olive oil	

PEEL AND GRATE THE potatoes to make approximately 3 cups. Rinse the shredded potatoes and squeeze dry.

Heat olive oil in a large skillet over medium-high heat. Make patties from the grated potatoes and place in the skillet. Reduce heat to medium low. Cook until browned on the bottom, about 7 to 8 minutes, then turn over. Sprinkle cheese over the hash browns and cook several minutes until melted. Makes 4 servings.

Anne Read
RIVER FARM

---

checking out chicory

Chicories are just beginning to appear in American salads. They can be broad-leaved or frilly, red or yellow, with fully developed heads or with tender mellow hearts. This diversity of textures and flavors come from these three types of chicory.

Endive: Frilly-leaved endive can be used in the leafy stage or allowed to form a head similar to iceberg lettuce. In the leafy stage, the leaf is slightly bitter with a sharp flavor. The developed heads have more of a mellow, buttery taste. Frisee is a popular variety with finely cut leaves. Endive adds a unique accent to salads and is wonderful in soups.

Escarole: Escarole is delicately crunchy with a milder bite to it than endive. The broad, flat lightly sweet leaves are similar in appearance to butterhead lettuce. An all-around great variety for planting, some varieties have even been known to survive temperatures down to 7°F. An essential ingredient in Italian salads.

Radicchio: A heading type of chicory, here in America the red type is generally thought of as radicchio, though they can be red or green. Piquant, crunchy and surprisingly bittersweet, radicchio is highly recommended and is quite popular grilled or broiled.

Sweet & Sour Oyster Mushrooms with Vegetables

Batter-dipped and fried oyster mushrooms with a sweet & sour pineapple stir-fry.

1/2 cup carrot discs
1/2 cup of 1-inch celery slices
1 cup sliced bell peppers
   (red and green mix)

Batter:

1 egg
1 cup water
1/4 teaspoon baking soda
1/4 teaspoon salt

1/2 medium onion, cut in 1-inch pieces
1/2 cup pineapple chunks
Sweet and sour sauce
   (store bought or home made)

1 1/3 cups flour
1/2 pound oyster mushrooms, cut
   in 2-inch pieces

MAKE BATTER BY beating egg with water, baking soda, and salt. Add flour, stir with fork but do not blend completely as the batter should remain lumpy. Dip oyster mushroom pieces in the batter, cook in oil until golden brown; drain.

Stir fry vegetables using a small amount of oil, then add mushrooms, pineapple, and sweet & sour sauce. Heat and serve over rice. Makes 4 servings.

Bob & Harriet Ames
SKUNK BAY MUSHROOMS

Low Fat Veggie Burritos

I like this recipe because it can also be served as a hot dip with tortilla chips.

3 16-ounce cans fat free refried beans
3 cloves garlic, crushed and pressed
1 medium onion, chopped
1 cup shredded carrots
1/2 cup diced celery
1/3 bunch fresh cilantro, chopped
1 4-ounce can diced green chiles
1 large potato, grated

2 large tomatoes, diced
1 28-ounce can stewed tomatoes
2 teaspoons cumin
1 teaspoon coarse pepper
Hot sauce to taste (about 1 tablespoon)
1 cup grated nonfat cheese
4 dozen small flour or corn tortillas
   (warmed)

Simmer 20 min

SIMMER ALL INGREDIENTS together except cheese and tortillas in deep soup pot for 20 minutes.

To assemble burritos: Put generous amount of bean mixture on one edge of tortilla. Add a sprinkle of cheese and fold like an envelope. Wrap individually with saran wrap and freeze on cookie sheet. Once frozen, store in large plastic bags in freezer. To serve, microwave 45 seconds on each side. Serve with salsa.

conventional oven?

Betty Rozier
PIKE MARKET SENIOR CENTER

---

fruit conversion chart

You may only need 2 cups of sliced pears for that tantalizing pear tart recipe you've been wanting to try, but just how many pears does it take to equal 2 cups? And, since fruit is often sold by the pound, how many pounds would it take to bake into a pie brimming with apples? Here's a handy chart to help simplify things a bit.

Apples 1 pound = 4 small, 3 medium, 2 large, 3 cups diced, 2-3/4 cups sliced

Apricots 1 pound = 12 fresh; dried apricots 1 cup = 28 large or 27 medium halves

Bananas 1 pound = 2 large, 3 medium, 4 to 6 small, 2 cups sliced, 1 1/2 cups diced, 1/3 cup mashed

Lemons 1 medium = 2 to 3 tablespoons juice, 2 to 3 teaspoons grated peel

Limes 1 medium = 1 to 2 tablespoons juice, 2 teaspoons grated peel

Oranges 1 medium = 1/2 cup bite-size pieces, 1/3 to 1/2 cup juice, 1 tablespoon grated peel

Peaches/ Nectarines 1 pound = 2 large, 3 to 4 medium, 2 cups sliced, 1-2/3 cups diced

Pears 1 pound = 2 large (Bartlett/D'Anjou size), 3 medium (Bosc size), 2-1/2 cups sliced

Plums 1 pound = 6 medium, 12 to 15 extra small, 2-1/2 cups sliced, 2 cups diced

Strawberries 1 pint basket = 3 cups whole, 2-1/4 cups sliced

Stuffed Melenzana

In Italy, eggplant is known as "melenzana".

1 medium eggplant
1 teaspoon chopped fresh basil
Salt and pepper to taste
2 cloves garlic, cut in half
Fontina cheese, diced

1/3 cup chopped prosciutto
Olio Santo* (spiced olive oil)
Marinara (or spaghetti) sauce
Italian bread crumbs

* Available through mail order or at the Pike Place Market.

PEEL EGGPLANT AND CUT 5 slits, leaving about an inch from each end intact. Sprinkle salt, pepper, and basil on the eggplant. Stuff each slit with garlic, cheese, and prosciutto.

Using Olio Santo, sauté eggplant on all sides until brown. Place eggplant in casserole dish. Pour in the marinara sauce, covering the eggplant. Sprinkle top with bread crumbs. Bake in a 400 degree oven for 35 minutes. Serves 2.

Kevin Roy
SOTTO VOCE

parsley benefits	Parsley packs a powerhouse of benefits, that is if you eat it instead of decorate your plate with it. In just four ounces of fresh parsley you'll get nearly twice as much vitamin C as in an orange, more beta carotene than a single carrot, several B vitamins, 20 times more iron than a serving of liver, and more calcium than a cup of milk. Plus parsley has been used as a diuretic, to expel excess gas, and help with digestion. And, when it comes to hay fever, parsley may just help. According to one study, parsley can inhibit histamines, the chemical produced by our bodies the sets off allergy symptoms.
	If there were such a thing as a "socially acceptable" herb, parsley would rank number one. It has a high chlorophyll content, the highest of any herb. What does that mean? Since chlorophyll is a natural breath freshener, that means parsley eaters are a socially acceptable group!

Garbanzo-Meatball Stew

Sounds good!

Now selling over 18 years at the Pike Place Market, Doris and husband Donald Mech of Mech Apiaries bring a wide range of honey and beeswax products.

This is a great meal to fix when you're certain of the exact dinner hour; or prepare most of the stew ahead of time for a quick fix fantastic stew.

1 1/2 pounds lean ground beef
2 tablespoons oil
1 15-ounce can tomato sauce
2 tablespoons honey
2 cloves garlic, minced
1 cup chopped onion

1 teaspoon salt (optional)
Fresh ground pepper to taste
2 15-ounce cans garbanzo beans, drained
3 cups diced fresh zucchini
1 cup diced fresh tomato

SHAPE THE GROUND BEEF in 1-inch balls and brown in a large skillet with the oil. Turn to brown on all sides. Remove meatballs from skillet and set aside. In the same skillet, stir together the tomato sauce, honey, garlic, onions, salt and pepper. Add the garbanzo beans, cover, and allow to simmer for 30 to 60 minutes.

Return meatballs to skillet mixture. Bring to simmering, adding just a little water if needed. Add the diced zucchini and diced fresh tomatoes, stirring gently. Cover again and cook over medium-low heat for about 10 minutes. Do not overcook the zucchini, it should be just slightly crisp. Serve immediately while piping hot. Make 4 to 6 generous servings.

Doris Mech
MECH APIARIES

Chicken and Oyster Mushrooms

A thick and creamy meaty sauce enhanced by the nutty flavor of Oyster mushrooms.

12 ounces chicken or turkey meat,
  cut into bite-sized pieces
1 1/2 cups heavy cream
1/2 cup chicken stock
1 tablespoon cream sherry
1 teaspoon fresh crushed garlic

1 tablespoon finely chopped onion
8 ounces fresh oyster mushrooms
3 tablespoons cornstarch
1/2 cup water
Salt and pepper to taste

CUT MUSHROOMS AND CHICKEN or turkey meat into 1 to 2-inch pieces. Cook chicken or turkey in a large skillet till done. Add cream, chicken stock, sherry, garlic, onion, and mushrooms. Heat over a medium heat till simmering. Reduce heat to low and simmer for an additional 5 minutes. Mix cornstarch and water together, then add to skillet, stirring constantly till thickened. Add salt and pepper to taste. Serve over toast, rice or noodles and garnish with chopped parsley. Makes 4 to 6 servings.

Bob & Harriet Ames
SKUNK BAY MUSHROOMS

Zucchini Bread

Fear zucchini no more. Shred several pounds of zucchini and freeze in 2 cup portions in Ziploc bags and make zucchini bread all year!

3 eggs
1 1/2 cups sugar
1 cup vegetable oil
2 teaspoons vanilla
2 cups packed, finely shredded
   unpeeled zucchini (one pound
   Alden Farms zucchini)

3 cups all-purpose flour
1 teaspoon baking powder
1 teaspoon baking soda
1 teaspoon salt
1 1/2 teaspoons cinnamon
1/2 teaspoon nutmeg
1/2 cup chopped walnuts

IN LARGE BOWL, beat eggs well. Gradually beat in sugar, then oil and vanilla. Stir in zucchini. In separate bowl, mix together flour, baking powder, soda, salt, cinnamon, and nutmeg. Stir into zucchini mixture along with nuts.

Pour batter into 2 greased 8 x 4-inch loaf pans. Bake at 350 degrees for 50 minutes or until tester inserted in center comes out clean. Let cool in pan for 10 minutes, then turn out onto rack to cool completely. Makes 2 loaves.

Jan Alden
ALDEN FARMS

Thumbprint Cookies

Each time you make these cookies, try a new herbal jelly and discover which one you like best.

2/3 cup sugar
2/3 cup butter
1 egg
1 teaspoon vanilla extract

1/4 cup finely chopped pecans
1 1/2 cups unbleached flour
1/2 teaspoon baking powder
3 tablespoons herbal jelly, lavender is great*

* Available through Rachel-Dee Herb Farm at the Pike Place Market

EITHER BY HAND OR food processor, mix sugar and butter till creamy. Add egg, vanilla, and pecans till mixed. Stir in flour and baking powder. Roll into 1-inch balls, using small amount of flour on hands to prevent stickiness. Place balls on greased cookie sheet about 1-inch apart. Press thumb onto each cookie, creating a well. Bake in preheated oven at 350 degrees for 8 minutes. Remove, fill well with jelly. Return to oven for an additional 3 minutes.

Ivonne Brown
RACHEL-DEE HERB FARM

Chocolate Covered Cherries

The Razey's are in their 5th generation of farming what is now over 7 different varieties of certified organic cherries growing on 1,000 trees, all picked by hand.

Chocolate covered cherries are simple, quite delicious and everyone's favorite.

Fresh ripe cherries
Melted chocolate chips

WASH CHERRIES IN running water, do not soak. Dry off thoroughly. Leave pits in and stems on for ease of dipping. Spread cherries on cookie sheet and freeze until hard, about 30 minutes. Remove from freezer and immediately dip in melted chocolate. Place on wax paper till chocolate hardens. Don't forget to eat some yourself before they disappear!

Mary Kay Razey
RAZEY'S ORCHARDS

> *"Behold the fool saith, "Put not all thine eggs in one basket," but the wise man saith, "Put all your eggs in one basket — and watch that basket!"*
>
> — Mark Twain, Pudd'nhead Wilson (1894)

Raspberry Shortcakes

Ben Craft and Gretchen Hoyt, along with their two children, grow an abundance of berries near the Canadian border. Raspberries are their primary crop, and they have them from June to October at the Pike Place Market. While you're there, try some of the vegetables, flowers, or vinegars and jams.

Quick to make, but the flavor goes on and on and on...

4 cups raspberries
Sugar

4 slices poundcake or French toast
1 cup heavy cream

RESERVE 1/2 CUP raspberries for garnish. Mash the remaining berries and add 2 tablespoons sugar, or to taste. Let stand for a minimum of 15 minutes.

Cut the poundcake slices horizontally into two layers. Whip the cream and add 2 teaspoons sugar, or to taste.

To assemble, arrange a slice of poundcake on each plate. Spoon half the sweetened berries over the cake slices and top with half of the whipped cream. Place the remaining cake slices over the whipped cream and spoon the remaining sweetened berries on top. Top with the remaining cream. Garnish with the whole reserved raspberries. Makes 4 servings.

Gretchen Hoyt
ALM HILL GARDENS

YUMMY APPLE SAGE PIE

Herbs have a way of really enhancing the flavor of foods, such as sage does with apples.

Pie crust recipe for 2 crust pie
1 jar apple sage jelly *
cup boiling water
1/3 cup cornstarch

3 cups sliced apples
1/4 to 1/2 stick butter, cut in 1/8-inch 1/2
  slices
1/4 cup finely minced fresh sage

* Available through Rachel-Dee Herb Farm at the Pike Place Market

ROLL OUT DOUGH from your favorite pie crust recipe and put bottom crust in pie pan. In mixing bowl, combine apple sage jelly and boiling water; stir well using whisk to blend together. Allow mixture to cool slightly, then add cornstarch; mix well. Stir in apples and pour mixture into pie shell. Dot with butter and sprinkle with fresh sage. Finish by covering with top layer of crust. Bake in preheated oven at 375 degrees about 40 to 45 minutes. Remove from oven and allow to cool 1 to 2 hours before serving. Serves 6 to 8.

Ivonne Brown
RACHEL-DEE HERB FARM

Chrisman Farms Rolled Cake

Chrisman Farms is located halfway between Portland and Seattle in a small fertile valley alongside the Chehalis River. All the fruit used in jam and jelly making is grown and hand picked on the farm. Family owned and operated, Chrisman Farms' jams and jellies are available at Pike Place Market in Seattle, Olympia Farmers' Market, and also through mail order.

Tender and delicious with fresh-picked berry flavor that takes you back to the sunny days of summertime fun.

5 eggs
2/3 cup sugar
1/4 teaspoon salt
1/2 cup sifted cake flour

3 tablespoons melted butter
1 teaspoon vanilla
1 cup Chrisman Farms Jelly or Jam (Blackberry or Raspberry are especially good)

COMBINE EGGS AND SUGAR in a large bowl, beat only until blended. Place over hot water and heat until slightly hot, about 140 degrees. Remove from heat and beat until mixture holds a soft peak.

Combine salt and flour and fold into egg mixture. Fold in butter, about a tablespoon at a time. Blend in vanilla. Pour batter into a large 10 x 15-inch pan lined with wax paper.

Bake in a preheated oven at 350 degrees for 15 to 20 minutes. Turn quickly onto towel sprinkled with powdered sugar. Remove paper and trim off crusts. Roll cake and let cool until you can handle the cake. Unroll, spread with jam of choice, roll again and cool. Just before serving, sprinkle with powdered sugar.

Dennis Chrisman
CHRISMAN FARMS

Festive Punch · Orange Cream Cheese Dip

Grilled Peaches with Raspberries

Organic Fruit Rolls · Dried Cinnamon Apples

Leroy's Apple Pancakes

Sweet Pickles · Sweet Relish · Cider Fruit Salad

Fresh Tomato Basil Salad · Greek Cabbage Salad

**Willie Green's Salad Mix
with Sun-Dried Tomato Balsamic Vinaigrette**

Curried Squash & Mushroom Soup

Veggie Scrambled Eggs · Sunburst Sauté

Pesto Potatoes · Stir Fry Pea Vines

Bok Choy & Carrot Sauté · Almost Eggplant Parmesan

Blueberry Sugar Muffins · Procrastination Pear-Ginger Bars

Hazelnut Chocolate Chip Cookies · Pumpkin Cookies or Bars

Hazelnut Raisin Bread · Bee-Sweet Banana Bread

UNIVERSITY DISTRICT FARMERS' MARKET

LOCATION:
University Heights Community Center
Corner of NE 50th & University Way NE
End of May thru October
Saturdays, 9:00 a.m. - 2:00 p.m.

NOW THE MOST SIGNIFICANT AGRICULTURAL EVENT TO HAPPEN IN SEATTLE IN YEARS, THE University District Farmers' Market began in 1993 as a grassroots community-based event organized by volunteers. Since the Market is strictly devoted to food, the Market now represents the largest variety of fresh produce available in the Seattle area.

Come enjoy all the splendor of Seattle's largest Farmers-Only Market. Every week, over 40 growers from all over Washington bring their just picked harvest to the U-District. There are lots of delicious fruits and vegetables and organic produce along with fresh juices, honey, eggs, baked goods, cheese, nuts, herbs, wild mushrooms and preserves. Fresh flowers are always in season including favorites like cosmos, dahlias, geraniums, gladiolus, irises, lilies, peonies, and sunflowers. And, make your gardening season complete with the fine selections of nursery plants found at the Market.

Gather lots of great gardening and composting information and enjoy the live entertainment. Stop, shop and hobnob with Seattle-area celebrity chefs at the special on-site cooking demonstrations. Join in the fun—sample and choose the best from special tomato, apple, and greens tasting events. Neighbors meet neighbors here. They sit, chat and take the time to smell the basil. The Market has become a great social catalyst for a large, diverse urban neighborhood.

Hosted by the University Heights Center and co-sponsored by the Greater University Chamber of Commerce, the University District Farmers' Market is a non-profit organization dedicated to bringing local farmers and their farm products into the University District neighborhood.

Festive Punch

Larry Rankin of Woodring Orchard is the only cider vendor at the University District Farmers' Market. You'll also discover homemade apple syrups and applesauce. Larry sells at half a dozen other farmers' markets on the west side of the mountains.

Cider works very well as a blend with practically any other juice or combination of juices. This makes a very refreshing breakfast drink or afternoon pick-up.

1/2 gallon cider
3 cups cranberry juice

3 cups orange juice
2 cups Sprite, 7-up, or Ginger Ale

COMBINE ALL THE ABOVE together in a pitcher or large bowl. Enjoy!

Larry Rankin
WOODRING ORCHARDS

Orange Cream Cheese Dip

Ben Craft and Gretchen Hoyt, along with their two children, grow an abundance of berries near the Canadian border. Raspberries are their primary crop, and they have them from June to October at the University District Farmers' Market. While you're there, try some of their vegetables and flowers, or vinegars and jams.

This is delectable as a dip for fresh Washington red raspberries.

1 8-ounce package cream cheese
4 tablespoons honey
3 tablespoons orange juice (adjust amount to create a creamy texture)

BLEND CREAM CHEESE with honey and orange juice until it reaches a smooth and creamy texture. Although you can mix this dip by hand, for best results use a food processor or blender.

Ben Craft and Gretchen Hoyt
ALM HILL GARDENS

watermelon varieties for the north	variety	days to maturity	size	flesh color	description
	Crimson Sweet	85	15-25 lbs	Deep red	Blocky-round, striped rind, high sugar
	Garden Baby	70	5-7 lbs	Red	Round, thin rind, short-vined type, compact
	Park's Whopper	70	5-8 lbs	Red	Round, 9-inch diameter, high in sugar
	Pony Yellow	75	5-8 lbs	Lemon yellow	Round, thin skinned with dark green stripes
	Sugar Baby	80	8-10 lbs	Red	Round, small seeds, can be trellised
	Sweet Favorite	86	10-15 lbs	Red	Oblong with dark stripes, good for north
	Tiger Baby	80	7-10 lbs	Pink/Red	Striped, round to slightly oval
	Yellow Doll	75	5-8 lbs	Yellow	Round with small seeds, very sweet

Note: These varieties have all performed well in the north. Small, round watermelons are known to many as "icebox" types. Yellow Doll has done well in areas with cooler summer nights.

Grilled Peaches with Raspberries

Located in the Frenchman Hills northeast of Royal City, Tonnemaker Family Orchard grows 44 acres of fruit trees and 2 acres in vegetables. Kurt Tonnemaker, a third generation farmer, says the rest of the farm produces hay, wheat, a few feeder calves and quarter horses.

Sooo good, it tastes like you're eating dessert for breakfast, or brunch, or dinner!

2 tablespoons brown sugar
2 tablespoons fresh lime juice
1 cup fresh raspberries

2 medium size fresh, unpeeled peaches,
   halved and pitted (about 10 ounces)
Vegetable cooking spray

COMBINE SUGAR AND LIME juice in a shallow dish; stir well. Add 1/2 cup raspberries and mash. Add peaches, turning to coat. Marinate at room temperature, cut sides down, 30 minutes to 1 hour. Remove peaches, reserving marinade.

Coat grill rack with cooking spray and place on grill over low to medium coals. Place peaches, cut side down on rack and cook 2 minutes. Turn peaches over; cook 15 minutes or until tender, basting once with half of reserved marinade. Remove peaches from grill. Stir remaining 1/2 cup raspberries into remaining marinade and spoon over peach halves. Serve warm. Serves 2 to 4.

TONNEMAKER FAMILY ORCHARD

Organic Fruit Rolls

Imagine succulent Red Haven peaches and exquisite Red Gold nectarines so huge and perfectly ripe. Certified Organic growers Rick and Marilynn Lynn of Rama Farms bring that vision into a reality at the University District Farmers' Market.

These tantalizing fruit rolls can be put in the freezer in Zip-lock freezer bags for long-term storage up to one year.

1 cup organic apples slices
2 cups organic peach or nectarines slices
1/4 cup water
1 teaspoon spice (cinnamon, nutmeg, coriander, etc.—this is optional)

BLEND FRUIT WITH water in blender or food mill until evenly blended. Pour onto plastic-lined drying racks. Dry at high heat in a dehydrator for 2 to 4 hours, then reduce heat to low and dry for 24 to 30 hours. (If your dehydrator doesn't have a thermostat, allow 2 days to dry.) Rotate trays if necessary. Remove from plastic wrap when leathery and reroll.

Rick & Marilynn Lynn
RAMA FARMS

UNIVERSITY DISTRICT FARMERS' MARKET

Dried Cinnamon Apples

On the east side of the mountains, Shirley Cox and her husband grow an enormous amount of cherries, peaches, nectarines, apples, walnuts, and tomatoes.

Makes a wonderful snack or apple pie without the crust!

Fresh apples, enough to fill dehydrator
1/4 cup cinnamon
1 cup sugar

CORE, PEEL, AND SLICE apples using an apple peeler/corer. Mix cinnamon and sugar together in a large pie plate. Drop apple slices in cinnamon/sugar mixture and cover to coat both sides. Arrange slices on trays and set at highest setting; dry about 8 hours.

Don't use a dehydrator with the heating element at the bottom. The sugar will drip down some and could cause a fire.

Shirley Cox
COX FRUIT

Leroy's Apple Pancakes

Look for Patricia Dauer of Cedarwood Farm during apple season. That's when she brings delicious apples like Cameos and Golden Delicious to the University District Farmers' Market.

Try this satisfying pancake served for brunch.

2 teaspoons butter or maragine
2/3 cup whole wheat flour
1/3 cup oat bran
1/3 cup sugar
3/4 cup milk
2 eggs

1/2 teaspoon vanilla
2 apples (Golden Delicious, Winesap, or
   other cooking variety)
2 tablespoons lemon juice
powdered sugar

HEAT OVEN TO 425 degrees. Melt 1 teaspoon of margarine in each of 2 glass pie pans. In a medium bowl, mix flour, bran, and sugar. Add milk, eggs, and vanilla; mix well then set aside. Slice and cube unpeeled apples. Pour batter evenly into both pie pans, then sprinkle apple cubes on top of batter. Bake for 20 to 25 minutes. Dribble 1 tablespoon lemon juice over each cake and sprinkle with powdered sugar. Serve warm and enjoy! Makes 2 cakes.

Patricia Dauer
CEDARWOOD FARM

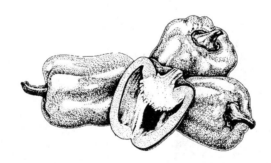

macro-nutrients	There are basic elements that are essential to the health and growth of plants. Carbon, hydrogen and oxygen are basic elements that mainly come from the air and water. But plants also need nitrogen, phosphorus, and potassium, known by their chemical symbols as N-P-K.

These elements are known as "macronutrients", so called because they are needed by plants in relatively large quantities. N-P-K provides the basic ingredients and building blocks for healthy plant growth. Nitrogen is vital to the process of plant cell growth and reproduction, resulting in a healthy vigorous plant. Since it's soluble, it's also the most deficient of the three.

Phosphorus increases the health and production of plants through improved disease resistance, root growth and fruit formation. Since it moves poorly through the soil, always mix it beneath the root zone before planting.

Potassium is also important for cell division and growth, plus it aids in the control and use of the nitrogen plants receive. And guess where there's an abundance of potassium? Over 41% of potash can be found in banana peel ash. Bananas anyone?

Sweet Pickles

Bob and Pat Meyer of Stoney Plains Farm have been with the market since day one. Bob took on organic farming after retiring from his 9-5 office job. Now he and his wife farm about 25 acres which includes assortment of vegetables and bedding plants. Though I hear that the Meyer's might soon be adding chicken eggs to that list.

Good on sandwiches or served as a condiment.

8 cups thinly sliced cucumbers
4 cups thinly sliced onions
2 small green peppers, chopped
2 tablespoons canning salt

2 cups dark vinegar or cider
3 cups sugar
2 teaspoons celery seed
2 teaspoons turmeric powder

COMBINE CUCUMBERS, ONIONS, and peppers in a large bowl. Sprinkle salt over the combination; let set for 30 minutes. In a large pot, bring vinegar, sugar, celery seed, and turmeric to a boil. Put cucumber mixture into liquid and simmer for 20 minutes over low heat. Put in hot jars and seal. Process in a boiling water canner for 10 minutes. Yields about 5 pints.

Bob and Pat Meyer
STONEY PLAINS FARM

Sweet Relish

Tasty, delicious, and always seems to disappear fast, so make enough to last you till next season!

3 dozen cucumbers, dill pickle size
4 large onions
3 red sweet peppers
3 green peppers
2/3 cup salt

1 quart cider vinegar
1 quart sugar
2 teaspoons celery seed
2 teaspoons black mustard seed

PUT CUCUMBERS, PEPPERS, onions, and salt through grinder. Move to a colander and let drain overnight. Bring cider vinegar, sugar, celery seed, mustard seed, and drained vegetables to a boil in a large pot. Put into pint jars and seal. Process in a boiling-water canner for 10 minutes. Yields 5 to 6 pints.

Bob and Pat Meyer
STONEY PLAINS FARM

Cider Fruit Salad

This is a no-sugar salad, so the fresh flavor of the fruit can really explode.

1/2 cup cold apple cider
2 ounces Knox Gelatin
1 cup boiling apple cider (can substitute
   1 cup ginger ale)
1 quart cold apple cider

1 cup grapes
1/2 cup chopped celery
1 cup cubed apples
1/2 cup crushed pineapple
1 tablespoon lemon juice

COMBINE 1/2 CUP cold cider and gelatin; soak for 10 minutes. Add mixture to 1 cup boiling cider, stir until gelatin is dissolved. In a large bowl, combine mixture with 1 quart cold cider. Add remaining ingredients once liquid begins to congeal. Pour into desired mold and refrigerate till set. Serves 8 to 10.

Larry Rankin
WOODRING ORCHARDS

Fresh Tomato Basil Salad

The freshest ingredients makes for an impressionable salad.

Slicing tomatoes, 1 per person. (Vine-
   ripened beefsteaks are a great choice)
Walla Walla sweet onions, finely diced
Fresh Italian Basil, finely minced

Freshly ground salt and pepper to taste
Sprinkling of raspberry vinegar

SLICE TOMATOES and place on platter. Sprinkle with onions, basil, salt and pepper. Add a dash of raspberry vinegar and serve freshly prepared.

Ben Craft and Gretchen Hoyt
ALM HILL GARDENS

Greek Cabbage Salad

John Huschle and Andrew Stout grow a huge variety of certified organic vegetables including a half a dozen types of lettuce, nearly 10 types of greens, a dozen different fresh herbs, and lots of exotic varieties that you just can't find in the supermarket. Look for their booth, Full Circle Farm, at the University District Farmers' Market.

A festive salad with a lot of flavor, great side dish for family picnics, pot-lucks, barbecue, or those hot summer days.

1 medium red cabbage
1 medium green cabbage (Early
   Jersey for best flavor)
1 red onion, diced
1 package feta cheese

1 1/2 cups raisins
1 cup toasted walnuts
1/4 cup toasted sesame oil
lemon juice to taste

CUT CABBAGE into 'slaw' style strips. Combine all ingredients together in a large serving bowl; toss, serve, and enjoy.

John Huschle & Andrew Stout
FULL CIRCLE FARM

---

peeling peppers perfectly

Hot peppers are a favorite, except maybe when it comes to peeling. Those tough skins should be removed if you're going to use the pepper fresh. By blistering the skin, it becomes easier to remove, and heat will help with that. You can even use the heat from your backyard barbecue grill.

When roasting peppers, avoid using charcoal lighter fluid, and if available, use wood charcoal instead of briquettes. Once the glowing coals are covered with a white ash, it's time to put on safety glasses. Chiles have been known to explode. Using tongs, lay peppers on the grill preferably close to the coals. Keep turning the peppers until they're blackened on all sides, then throw them for 5 minutes into a "sweat lodge", an open paper bag. Here the steaming action will help loosen the skin.

Once steamed, the skin will easily slide off under cold running water. Protect your hands with rubber gloves first to avoid that painful chile burn. If you carefully cut around the stem, the seeds and membranes should pull out willingly. Now you can use them in your favorite recipe, or toss into freezer bags where they will keep in the freezer for six months or longer.

Willie Green's Salad Mix with Sun-Dried Tomato Balsamic Vinaigrette

Jeff Miller became involved in organic farming to offer local consumers a chance to purchase healthy, organic produce, hence Willie Green's Organic Farm. Miller's goal is to educate consumers in the importance of eating organic in-season produce.

You can prepare a larger quantity, then refrigerate the unused portion.

8 ounces Willie Green's salad mix (available at the University District Farmers' Market)
4 tablespoons sun-dried tomato balsamic Vinaigrette (recipe follows)

For Vinaigrette mix
2 tablespoons olive oil
2 tablespoons balsamic vinegar
1 tablespoon sun-dried tomatoes, soaked until soft and then chopped
1 tablespoon red wine vinegar

1/4 teaspoon minced garlic
1/4 shallot, minced
1/4 teaspoon finely chopped fresh summer savory
1/4 teaspoon finely chopped fresh green basil

MIX ALL VINAIGRETTE ingredients in a shaker bottle. Shake and allow to sit at room temperature for 2 hours, shaking every 30 minutes. Sprinkle over Willie Green's Salad Mix. Serves 4.

Jeff Miller
WILLIE GREEN'S ORGANIC FARM

Curried Squash & Mushroom Soup

Jerry Goronea and Anne Read began River Farm in 1977. They use sustainable and soil-building techniques that imitate nature. Their biggest reward, seeing an organic system come alive, has also been their biggest challenge economically—in managing an organic approach. They sell at both Kittitas County and University District Farmers' Markets.

Take your time and allow this soup to simmer awhile to really blend its flavors.

2 acorn or butternut squash	1 clove garlic, crushed
2 1/2 cups water or stock	1/2 teaspoon coriander
1 cup orange juice	1/2 teaspoon cinnamon
2 tablespoons butter or margarine	3/4 teaspoon ground ginger
1/2 cup chopped onion	1/4 teaspoon dry mustard
Salt to taste	6 ounces mushrooms, sliced
1/2 teaspoon cumin	

CUT SQUASH LENGTHWISE, bake face down on oiled tray in 375 degree oven for 30 to 40 minutes. Discard seeds; scoop out inside pulp and put in blender with water or stock; puree till smooth. Combine puree in saucepan with juice.

Meanwhile, heat butter in skillet; add onion, garlic, salt, and spices. Sauté until onion is soft. Add mushrooms, cover and cook 10 minutes. Add sauté to squash puree; heat gently. Add few dashes cayenne.

Jerry Goronea & Anne Read
RIVER FARM

---

perfect pancakes

Equipment: You'll need a griddle of some sort, and there are many options to choose from. A well-seasoned black iron griddle is a favorite for many as are soapstone griddles (a bit more pricey). Non-stick griddles are also available, or an electric fry pan can be used.

Forming: For even-sized pancakes, use a soup ladle, big dipper, or glass measuring cup for dipping into batter and spreading on griddle. A big sturdy bowl with pouring spout can also be used, but is a bit harder to handle and measure out even portions.

Cooking: Use as little oil as possible. A non-stick cooking spray can be substituted. As you're making pancakes, you'll need to adjust the heat slightly as the surface temperature drops and then heats back up again.

From Pancakes to Hotcakes: Who likes to watch someone else eat pancakes while they're waiting for their own to cook? Keep a growing stack nice and hot for everyone to enjoy. As each pancake is done, put on an ovenproof plate in a 225 degree oven.

Veggie Scrambled Eggs

Michaele Blakely of Carnation, Washington is farming very close to the Urban fringe. Certified organic, she does a large variety of vegetables and herbs. Michaele is also referred to as "The Egg Lady", so guess what else she sells. Along with her eggs, she also takes special orders for chickens. Look for her booth, Growing Things.

Notice the yolks on free-range organic eggs. The flavorful yolks are a bright orange color as opposed to the pale yellow yolks from confined chickens.

6 free-range organic eggs	1/4 cup chopped bell pepper
1/4 cup milk	3 dashes Tabasco sauce
2 slices turkey bacon, sliced into strips	1 cup shredded cheese
1/4 cup sliced mushrooms	Salt and pepper to taste
1/4 cup chopped broccoli	Oil spray/olive oil

MIX EGGS AND MILK in medium size bowl. Sauté bacon in skillet over high heat for 1 minute, add veggies and a little olive oil. Stir until veggies are coated with oil, then lower heat to medium. Cook until veggies begin to soften. Lower heat, add eggs and Tabasco sauce. Stir occasionally until eggs are almost done, then add cheese. Continue stirring; add salt and pepper to taste. Serves 3 to 5.

Michaele Blakely
GROWING THINGS

Sunburst Sauté

Originating in 1995, the goals of Seattle Youth Garden Works are to grow great produce, create healthy gardens, a strong community, and provide opportunities for homeless youth in transition.

Sunburst squash is sometimes referred to as "pattypan" or "scallop". Try this delicious combination of mushrooms, mint, red peppers, and squash—a real "sunburst" of flavor.

3 tablespoons olive oil	4 to 6 medium sunburst squash
3 cloves garlic	8 to 10 mushrooms
1 medium onion	3 sprigs fresh mint
1 red pepper	

CUT VEGETABLES any way you like, but not very chunky or thick. Heat olive oil in skillet and cook garlic gently. Add onion, red pepper, and squash. When half cooked, add mushrooms and mint. Sauté on medium to high heat until onions and mushrooms are soft. Serves 4 as a side dish; 2 for a main meal.

SEATTLE YOUTH GARDEN WORKS

Pesto Potatoes

Kate and Bill Halstead of Rocky Prairie Herb Gardens sell a lovely variety of fresh culinary and medicinal herbs. They also bring along dried herbs too, like lavender, to the University District Farmers' Market.

Pesto is great in omelets, spread on grilled French bread, or mixed with a little cream for a quick, creamy sauce on pasta, fish, or vegetables.

1 to 2 pounds new potatoes, cut into small chunks
1/2 to 1 cup fresh basil pesto (recipe follows)
1/4 to 1/2 cup olive oil

BOIL OR STEAM potatoes until just tender when pierced with a fork. Pour into a baking dish at least 1 1/2-inches deep. Spoon mixture of pesto and olive oil over potatoes. Bake at 350 degrees for 20 to 30 minutes.

Barbecue alternative

Make a large foil dish that can be folded over to seal, and fill with the above mixture. Seal and place away from the center of your barbecue coals for at least 1/2 hour of main dish cooking time.

Basic Basil Pesto

2 cups fresh basil leaves
2 large cloves garlic
1/2 cup freshly grated Parmesan cheese

1/4 cup pine nuts, walnuts, or almonds
1/2 cup olive oil
Salt and freshly ground pepper to taste

Combine basil, garlic, cheese, and nuts in a food processor. When mixed well and with motor running, slowly add oil. Season to taste with salt and pepper. Toss with your favorite fresh cooked pasta. You can cover leftover pesto with a thin layer of olive oil if not being used immediately, or you can also freeze it.

Kate & Bill Halstead
ROCKY PRAIRIE HERB GARDENS

---

a perfect brew

Brew your own herbal teas gently to allow their flavors to develop just right. Always determine the strength or weakness of your tea by taste and not by sight. Here are some basic steps to help you brew the perfect pot of tea.

1. Release the herb's oils by bruising the leaves with your fingers. Put crushed herbs in tea balls, spoon-shaped tea infusers, or tea bags.

2. For each cup of hot water, add one teaspoon of dried herbs or one tablespoon of fresh herbs. (Adjust amounts to suit your taste.)

3. Pour boiling water over the tea ball, infuser, or bag in the teapot or cup.

4. Let it steep for four to six minutes (up to 10 minutes if using seeds or roots). Remove tea ball or bag.

5. Serve in cups and add lemon, honey, or other sweetener if desired.

Stir Fry Pea Vines

Members of the Hmong community, Tusong Thao of Tusong Thao's Farm originally began his extensive farming background in Southeast Asia. He grows a extensive variety of fresh vegetables, including a large selection of Asian greens, and lots of beautiful flowers.

That's right—pea vines are delicious too!

    1 pound pea vines, about one bundle, washed
    1/4 teaspoon salt
    1 tablespoon oyster sauce
    1 teaspoon oil

BLOT PEA VINES dry. Heat oil and salt over medium heat in skillet. When the oil is hot and popping, add pea vines and stir; pea vines will shrink. Sauté about 2 1/2 to 3 minutes. Serve hot and enjoy.

Tusong Thao
TUSONG THAO'S FARM

Bok Choy & Carrot Sauté

Bok Choy, pac choi, and pak choi are all the same names for a type of Oriental green having sturdy white or pale green leaf stems with buttery-textured slightly wavy green leaves.

1 bunch baby bok choy
1 small bunch carrots, 6 to 8-inches long
2 shiitake mushrooms
1 to 2 cloves garlic

2 tablespoons unsalted butter
Salt and pepper to taste
3 tablespoons chicken broth

CUT BOK CHOY in 1 to 2-inch pieces. Slice carrots diagonally 1/4-inch thick. Slice mushrooms 1/4-inch thick. Sauté mushrooms in 1 tablespoon butter until lightly browned; add garlic and stir. Add remaining butter with carrots and bok choy; stir over medium heat until carrots are tender. Add chicken broth, salt and pepper. Stir and bring to boil; serve hot. Serves 2 to 4.

Jeff Miller
WILLIE GREENS

Almost Eggplant Parmesan

Perhaps of all the vendors at the University District Farmers' Market, Billy Allstot travels the farthest, about a 5 hour drive just to get to the market! His customers make the trip worthwhile as they line up to buy his beautiful melons and incredible varieties of sweet and exotically hot peppers, tomatoes, and eggplant. His booth, Billy's, is a very popular booth at the University District Farmers' Market.

Some people like their eggplant cooked firm, others like it soft. Experiment to find your own taste preference.

2 sweet peppers, chopped
1 hot pepper, chopped (choose
   your favorite variety)
1 medium onion, chopped
1 to 3 cloves garlic, chopped
Olive oil
1 medium tomato, chopped

1 12-ounce can tomato paste
Water
Brown sugar to taste (start with 1 teaspoon)
Fresh basil, diced (start with 1 tablespoon)
Salt taste
1/8 teaspoon allspice
1 large eggplant, cut into 1/2 to 3/4-inch slices

Optional

Cheese of your choice
1 egg
1 pound cooked shrimp or country sausage

IN A LARGE SKILLET, sauté peppers, onion, and garlic in oil for a few minutes. Add tomatoes, tomato paste, and enough water to make a nice sauce; stir frequently. Add sugar, basil, allspice, and salt to taste; stir to combine then turn off heat.

Spread a thin layer of sauce in the bottom of a deep 8 x 10-inch casserole or dish. Place a single layer of eggplant on top of sauce, then a single layer of optional toppings. Layer sauce, eggplant, and optional toppings until all are used. Cover the top layer of eggplant with sauce and cover. Bake at 350 degrees for 15 minutes. Uncover and finish baking to desired consistency; about 15 to 30 minutes more. Serves 4 to 8.

Billy Allstot
BILLY'S

Blueberry Sugar Muffins

Farming near the Canadian border, the Benson family grows a tasty assortment of strawberries, raspberries, blueberries, marionberries, loganberries, and boysenberries for the University District Farmers' Market. They also bring home-made jams and toppings. It's no wonder with all those berries!

Light-textured muffins with the wildly fresh taste of blueberries.

1 cup sugar
1/2 teaspoon salt
1/2 cup shortening
3 eggs, beaten

2 cups flour
2 teaspoons baking powder
1 cup milk
3/4 cup fresh blueberries

WORK SUGAR AND SALT into shortening in a large bowl until well blended. Stir in eggs. Sift flour and baking powder together; stir into batter. Gradually add milk, stirring until dough is smooth and satiny. Fold in blueberries.

Pour batter into well-greased (or spray with non-stick coating) muffin tins, about 3/4 full. Bake in preheated 400 degree oven for 15 to 20 minutes, or until toothpick inserted in middle comes out clean. Makes 1 dozen.

The Benson Family
ERNIE'S BERRIES

Procrastination Pear-Ginger Bars

In a far, far distant place near Carltan, Washington, a young woman created Booth Canyon Orchard, growing an assortment of certified organic European pears. Bosc, Bartlett, and D'Anjou are her specialties, and case sales are available too.

I made this by accident one gray March day when I decided to put off my pruning chores.

1/2 cup butter
1/2 cup brown sugar
1 egg
1/2 cup molasses
2 cups whole wheat flour
1 teaspoon ground ginger
1 to 2 teaspoons grated fresh ginger

1 teaspoon cinnamon
1/4 teaspoon cloves
1/4 teaspoon salt
1 1/2 teaspoons baking powder
1/4 teaspoon baking soda
3/4 cup milk
3 to 5 ripe D'Anjou Pears, peeled and diced

CREAM TOGETHER butter and brown sugar in a large bowl. Beat in egg and molasses. In a separate bowl, sift together flour, spices, salt, baking powder and soda. Add flour mixture to butter mixture, alternating with a total of 3/4 cup milk. Beat till smooth.

Spread batter into a greased (or spray with non-stick coating) 9 x 12-inch pan. Arrange diced pears on top of batter. Bake in a preheated 350 degree oven for 10 to 15 minutes. Cut into bars and serve.

BOOTH CANYON ORCHARD

Hazelnut Chocolate Chip Cookies

Gerald Holmquist is a large grower of hazelnuts, and he brings them roasted, toasted, salted, in quick breads and cookies—any way you like 'em. Even plain in the shell. Speaking of shells, Holmquist Hazelnut Orchards has plenty and sells them bulk at the University District Farmers' Market and Pike Place Market. They make great mulch!

Grandma Holmquist has been making these cookies for many years, and generously hands them out to her hardworking clan. They are an all-time family favorite. Toasting the hazelnuts is an important step, as it draws out the nut's characteristic flavor. It's one of those simple techniques that yields big results and shouldn't be skipped.

2 eggs
1 1/2 cups firmly packed brown sugar
1/2 cup white sugar
1 cup canola or Wesson oil
2 teaspoons vanilla extract

1 teaspoon salt
1 teaspoon baking soda
2 1/2 cups flour
1 cup lightly toasted hazelnuts, chopped
1 cup chocolate chips

PREHEAT OVEN TO 350 degrees. In a large bowl, beat eggs well. Add sugars and beat until well-blended and smooth. Add oil and vanilla. Sift in dry ingredients; add hazelnuts and chocolate chips. Drop by rounded teaspoons onto cookie sheet. Bake in batches in the middle of oven for 8 to 10 minutes, or until the cookies are lightly browned. Makes about 48 cookies.

HOLMQUIST HAZELNUT ORCHARDS

Pumpkin Cookies or Bars

About 60 miles north of Seattle, Joanie McIntyre and Mike Shriver grow a large assortment of certified organic produce at their place, Rent's Due Ranch. A family farm which includes their children, they bring a variety of vegetables, glorious sunflowers, fantastic corn, and plenty of vegetable starts to the University District Farmers' Market. Many in the area know their quality produce from the Puget Sound Consumers Coop (PCC stores).

All the goodness of whole grains, pumpkin, nuts and dried fruit baked into a quick and tasty snack.

1 1/4 cups whole wheat flour
5 tablespoons soy flour or unbleached
   white flour
1 teaspoon salt
1/2 teaspoon cinnamon
1/2 teaspoon nutmeg
1/4 teaspoon cloves
1/2 cup butter

1/3 cup honey
1 egg
1 cup cooked and pureed pumpkin or
   any winter squash
1 cup chopped walnuts
1/2 cup raisins*
1/2 cup chopped dates*

* Or substitute with chocolate chips

STIR THE DRY ingredients and spices together in a bowl. In a separate large bowl, cream the butter and honey; beat in egg until smooth, then stir in pumpkin puree. (Don't worry if the texture looks strange.) Add the dry ingredients to the pumpkin mixture; blend together. Stir in nuts, dried fruit and/or chocolate chips.

Drop by heaping tablespoons full onto an oiled cookie sheet. Bake at 325 degrees for 15 minutes or until cookies are golden. Cool on a wire rack.

For pumpkin bars

Perform steps 1 through 4 above. Then pour batter into an oiled 8 x 8-inch pan. Bake at 325 degrees for 20 to 25 minutes or until done. Cool and cut into squares.

Joanie McIntyre & Mike Shriver
RENT'S DUE RANCH

---

the buzz about bees

Colonies can house from 30,000 to 50,000 bees in manmade hives, in fallen limbs, or in hollow trees. A good hive will produce 100 to 150 pounds of honey, but half of that should be left to feed bees during winter and maintain hive health.

Worker bees (undeveloped females) do most of the work; gathering pollen and nectar, building comb cells, feeding the queen and drones, processing honey and protecting the hive. No wonder their summer life-span is only about 6 weeks!

Drones are male bees whose main function is to mate with the queen bee. They also help maintain hive temperature for brood development. Larger and thicker than worker bees with a louder buzz, they're easy to tell apart from the others. They have no organs to gather honey and they also have no stinger.

The Queen. She reigns over the social order of the colony, inhibiting or stimulating certain behaviors by passing on a pheromone that she secretes. The queen can lay between 1,000-2,000 eggs a day from March until October. She lives about 2 years.

Hazelnut Raisin Bread

Hazelnuts are shorter and rounder than filberts, but both come from the same species of tree or bush. They can be used interchangeably in recipes.

1 egg
1 cup brown sugar
3 tablespoons oil
1 1/2 cups buttermilk
1 cup whole wheat flour
2 cups sifted flour

1 tablespoon baking powder
1/2 teaspoon baking soda
1 teaspoon salt
1 cup chopped hazelnuts
1 cup raisins

BEAT EGG UNTIL LIGHT; add brown sugar and beat until creamy. Add oil and buttermilk; beat to blend well. In a separate bowl, combine and sift dry ingredients; stir in hazelnuts and raisins. Blend dry ingredients into wet ingredients. Pour into greased and floured 9 x 5 x 3-inch pan. Bake at 350 degrees for 1 hour or until done. Make 1 loaf.

HOLMQUIST HAZELNUT ORCHARDS

Bee-Sweet Banana Bread

Willis Honey House is about 30 miles south of Seattle. They specialize in a tasty selection of flavored honeys and honey related products including beeswax candles.

Use a mild, light-colored honey for best banana flavor. Blackberry honey is also excellent.

1/2 cup honey	1/2 cup quick cooking rolled oats
1/3 cup butter or margarine	1 teaspoon baking powder
1 teaspoon vanilla	1 teaspoon ground nutmeg
2 eggs	1/2 teaspoon salt
3/4 cup whole wheat flour	1 cup mashed ripe bananas
1/2 cup all purpose flour	1/2 cup chopped walnuts

CREAM HONEY AND BUTTER in large bowl with electric mixer until fluffy. Beat in vanilla. Add eggs, one at a time, beating well after each addition. Combine dry ingredients in small bowl. Add to honey mixture alternately with bananas, blending well. Stir in walnuts.

Spoon batter into greased and floured 9 x 5 x 3-inch loaf pan. Bake in preheated 325 degree oven for 50 to 55 minutes, or until a wooden toothpick inserted near the center comes out clean. Cool pan on a wire rack for 15 minutes. Remove bread from pan; cool completely on wire rack. Makes 1 loaf.

WILLIS HONEY HOUSE

pickling chart

Keep in mind that when you are canning, processing time can change depending on the altitude of where you live. Listed are some guidelines for favorite pickling recipes. Refer to a canning book or contact your local Master Food Preserver extension agent with any questions you may have on canning.

Product	Style	Jar size	Minutes of process time at altitudes of			
			0-1,000	1,001-3,000	3,001-6,000	Above 6,000 ft
Dill pickles	Raw	Pints	10	15	15	20
		Quarts	15	20	20	25
Quick Dills	Raw	Pints	10	15	15	20
		Quarts	15	20	20	25
Quick Sweet pickles	Hot	Pints or quarts	5	10	10	15
	Raw	Pints or quarts	15	20	20	25
Bread and Butter pickles	Hot	Pints or quarts	10	15	15	20
Sweet Gherkin Pickles	Raw	Pints	5	10	10	15
Pickled Asparagus	Raw	Pints or quarts	10	15	15	20
Pickled Dilled Beans	Raw	Pints	5	10	10	15
Pickled Beets	Hot	Pints or quarts	30	35	40	45
Pickled Hot Peppers	Raw	Half-pints or pints	10	15	15	20
Pickle Relish	Hot	Half-pints or pints	10	15	15	20

Source: OSU Extension Service

Flavored Vinegars · Columbia Gold Marinade

Mennonite Green Tomato Pickles

Spicy Salsa Preserves · Iced Tomato Lime Soup

Fabulous Fresh Garlic Version of Grilled Shiitakes

Minted Carrots · Gingered Carrots

Mexican Potato No-Egg Salad

Zucchini Casserole

Columbia Gold Barbecue Sauce

Salmon Ala Columbia Gold · Golden Sunrise Chicken

Canned Apple Pie Filling · Peach Cobbler

Farm Fresh Apple Roly-Poly

My Mom's Tomato Soup Cake

Peanut Brittle

VANCOUVER FARMERS' MARKET

LOCATION
Downtown Vancouver on 5th & Broadway
April thru October
Saturdays, 9:00 a.m. - 3:00 p.m.

LOCATED IN VANCOUVER'S OLD TOWN HISTORIC DISTRICT, THE VANCOUVER FARMERS' Market is overflowing with some of the freshest quality produce around. Both familiar favorites and hard to find specialty items can be found at the Market. When spring arrives it's the best time for anyone to find their favorite heirloom plant for the garden. Come summer, heirloom vegetables with that one of a kind taste are in abundant supply. You'll even discover a variety of processed and specialty food items, and our much in demand hydroponic tomato grower brings fresh ripe tomatoes throughout the Market season.

Every Saturday at 10:00 a.m. cooking demonstrations are presented from chefs from some of the finer restaurants in town. They'll show you how to use local produce and prepare it to its fabulous best. And for fish that you can't get any fresher unless you catch it yourself, our local fish vendor brings in seasonal snapper, tuna, crab, and whole salmon, all custom cut for you right there at the market.

Vancouver is home to the oldest producing apple tree in the West and host to the ever popular Apple Tree Festival held the first Saturday in October. There's live music that the whole family can enjoy, and two special market days just for children where they can sell their own produce or crafts. It gives our kids a chance to try their hands at business and become young entrepreneurs.

Flavored Vinegars

If you want to know where to buy fresh herbs and an assortment of colorful dried flowers beautifully arranged at the Vancouver Farmers' Market, just ask for "Kinda Sorta". That's where you'll find Linda Noga's artistic creations of baskets, swags, wreaths, and arrangements.

It's easy to make your own flavored vinegars. All you need to do is choose which vinegar and which herbs you would like to use.

Choose Your Vinegar

Grocery stores are stocked with several types of vinegar; Red and White Wine, Balsamic, Rice, Cider, Distilled, and Malt. The quality of vinegar available varies greatly depending on the method of production.

The quality and flavor of the vinegar you buy really does matter, even when you are going to flavor it at home with herbs, spices, and fruit. Although, this doesn't mean you must buy a premium vinegar. Knowing about vinegar will give you the quality product you want to use for yourself and gift-giving.

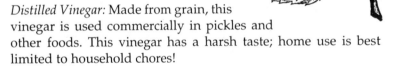

Distilled Vinegar: Made from grain, this vinegar is used commercially in pickles and other foods. This vinegar has a harsh taste; home use is best limited to household chores!

Cider Vinegar: Cider has many uses in cooking, from salad dressing to pickling. This vinegar has a fruity flavor. It can be used with medium or strong flavored herbs and spices. Choose a cider vinegar made from apples, not artificially flavored. Read the label!

Wine Vinegar: Wine vinegar is made from wine; red, white, or rose. Best and most economical vinegar for flavoring at home, with the white used for the lighter herbs (like French tarragon) and seasonings, and the red for the more robust flavors.

Rice Vinegar: Originally from the Chinese, rice vinegar has a mild, slightly sweet flavor. It is usually made from rice wine and comes in different forms. White rice vinegar is actually a pale golden color and enhances sweet and sour dishes. It is available plain or seasoned with salt and sugar. Buy the unseasoned; it is often less expensive and you can season it yourself if a recipe calls for seasoned rice vinegar. Rice vinegar combines well with peanut and sesame oils for salad dressings, sweet/sour soups and noodle dishes. Because of its mild taste, it works well for flavoring with delicate herbs and flowers.

Balsamic Vinegar: Brown in color and with an intense fruity aroma, this sweet-sour vinegar is made from grapes. The true Balsamic comes from the region of northern Italy where it has been made since the 11th century.

General Rules For Vinegar

- A bad vinegar will not improve with flavoring; use a good quality vinegar.

- Acidity should be at least 5%.

- Homemade vinegar should not be used for canning.

- When heating vinegar to a simmer, use a stainless steel pan. Aluminum will give the vinegar an off-flavor.

Choosing Herbs

Freshly picked, homegrown herbs yield the best results. If you didn't grow the herbs yourself, then check for freshly picked herbs at your local farmers' market or specialty food store.

For best results, pick herbs in the morning after the dew (or rain) has dried. Clean under running water and gently dry by patting with a clean towel.

Making Flavored Vinegars

- Containers for the steeping process can be any non-reactive material, such as glass, plastic, porcelain, or pottery. If using canning jars, place a piece of plastic wrap over the opening before putting on the metal lid.

- Cleanliness is essential. Wash all utensils, bottles, and containers with hot soapy water, then rinse in hot water.

- Use a variety of herbs, garlic, chili peppers, or one single herb. Use about 3 to 4 sprigs to each pint of vinegar. Be sure to completely immerse herbs so mold growth doesn't occur.

- Vinegar should be heated to a simmer (180 degrees) before adding herbs. Do not bring to a boil.

- Sample the vinegar after a couple of weeks. Usually the greatest amount of flavor is extracted after a month. Fruit vinegar is often ready in a week. Keep flavored vinegar in a dark place at room temperature while steeping. Stir or shake occasionally. Once the flavor is to your liking, strain the vinegar.

- Either line a strainer with a triple layer of cheesecloth, a single layer of muslin, a nylon jelly bag, or use a coffee filter in a drip holder. Repeat straining if needed.

- After straining, use a funnel to pour the vinegar into clean glass bottles. Fill to the top and add a sprig or two of the fresh herb.

Capping

If using corks, seal them with wax and ribbon. Melt paraffin or sealing wax in an empty tin or can placed in a pan of water over low heat. Cut a 4-inch length of ribbon and place it over the corked bottle. Holding the ribbon firmly, dip the corked top of the bottle an inch or two into the melted wax. Let it cool, then repeat the process until the wax is thick.

Labels

When the bottles are filled and capped, apply labels. These can be as simple or elaborate as you want. Office supply stores have a selection of plain self-adhesive labels in different sizes. Herb, kitchen supply, and housewares stores offer a wide range of decorative labels. If you are artistic, you may want to create your own labels. Felt-tip pens offer a range of colors, including gold and silver.

---

drought resistant plant quiz

What plant genus has all of the following characteristics?

- Leaves emit a pungent odor when crushed.

- Over 500 species found worldwide.

- Often used in floral displays.

- Sometimes used in food flavoring.

- Over 50 different species and cultivars found in various nurseries in the western United States.

- Some cultures rely on the curative values of this genus.

- Is very drought tolerant.

Congratulations if you guessed the genus *Salvia*, more commonly known as sage. Plant nurseries have developed many cultivars to enhance the quantity or color of blooms, plus other desirable traits of the original parent plant. Here's a look at three perennial Salvia species (USDA Zones 4 and up) that will make an impressive display in your garden with minimal effort and water.

Salvia azurea grandiflora grows well in all climates except the hottest deserts. A small shrub that grows to a maximum height of three to five feet, it's particularly showy with mass blooms of gentian blue all summer long right up to the first fall frost. Perhaps its only negative feature is that is sometimes will not survive poorly drained soils in wet winter areas. This species of sage is also sold as *Salvia pitcheri*.

Salvia officinalis (common sage) and its several cultivars will grow well in practically any area. All varieties are good for seasoning, and will usually grow three to four feet in height. Beware of the cultivar "Berggarten" unless you want its unique characteristics. Berggarten has the longest flavorful leaves, which makes it a best choice for culinary use, but is also non-blooming. Other cultivars have been developed for unique colors of leaves and flowers.

Salvia superba and its cultivars grow well in all Western climate zones and is hardy to Zone 4 in other parts of the country. Like most Salvias, this plant grows to a minimum height of three feet, but is more erect than other sages. Leaves are narrow with slender erect flowers topping each vertical stalk. Flowers are violet, blue, or purple as determined by the cultivar that your nursery may offer. The variety "Blue Hills" is nearly everblooming while other cultivars have special characteristics.

Ed Reed's southern California garden now totals over 400 different species of drought-resistant plants.

Recipes

When giving a bottle of flavored vinegar as a gift, consider writing a recipe for its use on a small card and tying it around the neck of the bottle. A gift basket might include several bottles of vinegar.

Storage

Don't keep your beautiful bottles of flavored vinegars in a sunny window if you plan to use them. They are best kept in a dark place at a cool temperature. Date the bottles. Flavored vinegars will keep up to a year, possibly longer, if stored in proper containers in a cool dark place, although for best flavor use within 6 months. Fruit vinegars should be used within 3 to 6 months. If a vinegar has mold floating on its surface, throw it away.

Fruit Vinegars

I freeze the berries in the summer and save them for the fall when I have more time to make vinegar. Some are slightly sweetened, most are not. Try all types of berries; raspberry, blackberry, huckleberry, blueberry, and strawberry all make delicious vinegar. Use 1 to 1 1/2 pounds of ripe berries for each quart of vinegar.

Linda Noga
KINDA SORTA

Columbia Gold Marinade

Gary Carr is a saucy kind of guy—in fact he produces three flavors of tantalizing barbecue sauce for Columbia Gold BBQ Sauce Company. Taste his own one-of-a-kind recipes at the Vancouver Farmers' Market.

A intriguing medley of barbecue sauce, beer, orange juice, and celery seed.

15 ounce bottle Columbia Gold BBQ Sauce
1 can of your favorite beer
1/2 cup juice from freshly squeezed orange
1 tablespoon celery seed

COMBINE ALL INGREDIENTS together and use to marinate your favorite meat or vegetables.

Gary Carr
COLUMBIA GOLD BBQ SAUCE COMPANY

Mennonite Green Tomato Pickles

Missy and Mike Stucky did a complete turn-around when they left their executive careers in Silicon Valley to start anew with Millennium Farms. Now they grow and specialize in organic and heirloom vegetables, especially tomatoes and peppers. Bring the kids in October to get a first-hand look at the unique pumpkins they grow called "Cinderella Pumpkins."

Here is a great recipe to use for all those late fall green tomatoes that just won't have time to ripen.

1 gallon green tomatoes, slice thin
8 small onions (baby size)

1 each red & green bell pepper, chopped
1/2 cup salt

Combine together for the syrup:
3 cups vinegar
2 cups water
1 teaspoon celery seed
1 1/2 teaspoons turmeric

1/2 teaspoon whole cloves
2 tablespoons mustard seed
5 cups sugar

COMBINE TOMATOES, ONIONS, bell peppers, and salt. Add ice cubes to weigh down and allow to soak for 3 hours; then drain.

Add mixture of drained vegetables to the syrup and bring to boiling point but do not boil. Ladle into hot canning jars and seal. Process in a boiling-water canner for 15 minutes. Makes 8 to 10 pints.

Missy & Mike Stucky
MILLENNIUM FARMS

Spicy Salsa Preserves

Try this fresh salsa to help liven up those dreary winter days.

3 pounds of tomatoes, peeled and
   coarsely chopped (about 7 cups)
2 cups sugar
1 1/2 cups chopped green bell peppers
1/2 cup fresh lime juice

1 teaspoon grated lime peel
1 teaspoon ground cumin
1 teaspoon salt
1/2 teaspoon ground red pepper

COMBINE ALL INGREDIENTS in a large saucepan. Bring to a boil; reduce heat to medium. Cook, uncovered, stirring occasionally until thickened, about 1 1/4 hours. Refrigerate in a covered container up to 2 months, or ladle into canning jars and process according to manufacturer's instructions. Makes about 4 pints.

Missy & Mike Stucky
MILLENNIUM FARMS

---

grow a rainbow of tomatoes

If you want to add some color to your garden, try growing one of today's exotic tomatoes and you'll find more than just gold at the end of the rainbow. Actually, the tomato wasn't always red. When the fruit first arrived in Italy it was well-received as a "golden apple". Records describe a yellow tomato crop in Thomas Jefferson's garden at Monticello.

Tomatoes also come in colorful hues of white, yellow, red, orange, green, purple, chocolate brown, and even multicolored stripes. Here are some of the exotic ones that I like best:

Black Prince A rich chocolate-mahogany color, this tomato has an earthy flavor.

Green Zebra These three-ounce fruits ripen to a sweet amber green striped with dark green.

Pineapple A large, colorful tomato with a tropical, fruity flavor. The meaty flesh is streaked with red and yellow, both inside and out.

Pruden's Purple An early, purple tomato with a creamy texture and delicious flavor.

Sausage Its name describes only its unique shape. This red tomato is also long on flavor, and a sure standout in salads or sauces.

Snow White A pale yellow, sweet cherry tomato just right for the Seven Dwarfs.

Tangerine This one is noted for its meaty texture and deep yellow-orange brilliance.

Try these tomatoes to add some color to your cooking and eating, and grow a rainbow of these varieties in your garden.

Iced Tomato Lime Soup

To retain the unique slushy nature of this soup, serve it in clear glass bowls over crushed ice. Swirl the top of each bowl with pesto and place a spring of fresh basil on the ice.

1 large onion, chopped	1 tablespoon minced fresh thyme
2 tablespoons chopped shallots	1/2 teaspoon sugar, or to taste
1 tablespoon butter	Salt and freshly ground pepper to taste
6 large tomatoes; peeled, chopped, and seeded	3/4 cup heavy cream
3/4 cup chicken broth	1/3 cup sour cream
1 tablespoon tomato paste	Juice of 1 large lime (about 4 tablespoons)
	Dash of Tabasco sauce

SAUTÉ THE ONION and shallots in butter, covered, until soft but not browned. Add tomatoes, chicken broth, tomato paste, thyme, sugar, salt and pepper. Cover and simmer 20 minutes; remove from heat and allow to cool.

Transfer mixture into food processor. Add cream, sour cream, lime juice and Tabasco; puree until smooth. Cover and place in freezer for 2 hours. Add seasonings if necessary and serve garnished with lime slices. Makes 6 servings.

Missy & Mike Stucky
MILLENNIUM FARMS

The Fabulous Fresh Garlic Version of Grilled Shiitakes

Located in Husum, Washington, Mike Rachford of Monarch Gourmet Mushrooms has become a very popular vendor at the Vancouver Farmers' Market. He sells chanterelles in season as well as shiitake mushrooms and growing kits.

Add a special touch by brushing the cap side of the grilled mushroom with barbecue sauce.

1 pound large fresh shiitakes	1/4 cup chopped parsley
1/2 cup butter, melted	1/2 teaspoon freshly ground pepper
4 cloves garlic, minced	1/4 teaspoon salt

REMOVE STEMS FROM mushrooms; discard stems. Combine butter along with garlic, parsley, pepper and salt; spread evenly on both sides of cap. Cook mushrooms, without grill lid, over medium-hot coals (350 to 400 degrees) about 8 minutes, turning once. Yield: 4 servings.

Mike Rachford
MONARCH GOURMET MUSHROOMS

Minted Carrots

Mint lovers will surely love these tender carrots flavored with fresh mint.

5 to 6 carrots, sliced
1/4 cup butter, melted
1 teaspoon sugar

1/2 teaspoon salt
1 tablespoon chopped fresh mint leaves

BOIL OR STEAM CARROTS until tender. Drain. Put drained carrots in a serving bowl. Add the remaining ingredients and toss well to coat carrots. Serves 4.

Missy Stucky
MILLENNIUM FARMS

soup side-kicks	*Clear Soups:* crisp crackers, cheese pastry, toasted sourdough bread, garlic croutons, cheese dumplings.
	Cream Soups: potato chips, seeded crackers, pretzels, cheese puffs, slivered almonds, bite-sized Shredded Wheat.
	Bean Soups: chips, salsa, pesto, avocado, olives, cheese bread sticks, saltine crackers, cheese popcorn, Triscuits.
	Chowders and Meat Soups: oyster crackers, Melba toast, bread sticks, toasted garlic bread, Oriental noodles, sautéed wheat berries.

Gingered Carrots

The fresh flavor of carrots take on a new character when heightened by ginger and cinnamon.

5 to 6 carrots, sliced
1/4 cup melted butter
1 tablespoon brown sugar

1/2 teaspoon salt
1/4 teaspoon ginger
1/8 teaspoon cinnamon

BOIL OR STEAM CARROTS until tender, then drain. Put drained carrots in a serving bowl. Add the remaining ingredients and toss well to coat carrots. Serves 4.

Missy Stucky
MILLENNIUM FARMS

grains glossary

Barley: *Whole barley* has a nutty, chewy texture; also called hulled barley, pot barley, or Scotch barley. Usually sold in specialty or natural foods stores. Pearled barley has had the hull and bran removed, leaving a polished, white kernel. Widely available in supermarkets. *Malted barley* is a powder made by sprouting and pulverizing the grain. Malted barley is also the main ingredient in beer and malt whiskey.

Buckwheat: Botanically a fruit but used as a grain, kernels (called groats) can be roasted, unroasted, or ground into flour. *Kasha* has a nutty flavor and comes from roasted buckwheat groats. Strong-flavored, highly nutritious grain.

Bulgur: Also known as wheat pilaf or parboiled wheat, bulgur is precooked and dried cracked wheat. Similar to cracked wheat but cooks faster and has a slightly nuttier taste.

Cornmeal: Ground corn from dried yellow or white kernels.

Cracked wheat: Coarsely ground whole wheat kernels. Can be used in place of whole wheat grains, but cooks faster.

Hominy grits: Hulled and dried coarsely ground corn lacking the bran and germ of the whole kernel. Sold dried (soak before cooking) or canned.

Millet: Bland but crunchy texture similar to poppy seeds, sold whole and cracked. Tiny yellow kernels used in cakes, cookies, breakfast cereals, bread puddings, and as a rice substitute. Commonly used in bird seed mixes.

Oats: Once thought of as a useless weed, now a popular grain used in cookies, desserts, and breakfast cereals. Oats do not contain gluten, a necessary protein that works with yeast to make bread dough rise. *Whole oats*, called groats, contains the whole grain (minus the outer hull); the bran, germ, and endosperm. *Rolled oats* (the most common form) are flakes of steamed and flattened unpolished oat kernels. *Quick-cooking oats* are thin precut, steamed and flattened even more than rolled oats. *Instant rolled oats* are quick oats with the thickening substance, guar gum, added.

Mexican Potato No-Egg Salad

A young mom and Northwest native, Amy Blankenship lives on a small family farm where they still do things the old-fashioned way—growing, canning, and preserving their own food. Amy is the Market Assistant for the Vancouver Farmers' Market.

Standard potato salad takes a new taste adventure with zesty dressing, tomatoes, and olives.

6 medium potatoes, boiled until tender
2 large firm tomatoes, cut into bite-sized
   pieces

1 can olives
1 each green & yellow pepper, cut into
   bite-sized pieces

Combine for dressing:
1 package taco seasoning mix
2 tablespoons rice vinegar
2 tablespoons canola oil
pinch of dill weed

CUT COOLED COOKED potatoes into bite-sized pieces. Put potatoes, tomatoes, olives, and peppers into serving bowl and toss well with dressing. Chill for 2 to 3 hours or prepare the day before. Serves 4 to 6.

Amy Blankenship
VANCOUVER FARMER'S MARKET ASSISTANT

---

more grains glossary

Rice: A grain that grows in water, available in long, short, or medium-length grains. (The shorter the grain, the more it will cling together when cooked.) *Brown rice* has a nutlike flavor and chewy texture, and contains the bran and germ of the kernel. *White rice* is milled and polished rice kernels with bran and germ removed during processing, leaving only the starchy endosperm. *Converted (parboiled)* rice is steamed and pressurized brown rice that is then milled and polished into white rice. Since the steam pressure forces the nutrients from the bran and germ into the endosperm, converted rice is more nutritious than white rice. *Instant rice* (precooked and dehydrated white rice) is lower in minerals than all other kinds of rice. *Wild rice* is not a true member of the rice family, but comes from the seeds of an aquatic grass.

Rye: A nutritious cereal grain that's low in gluten. Available as whole or cracked rye kernels.

Triticale: A cross between wheat and rye, available as grain or flour.

Wheat berries: These are whole-wheat grains, unpolished whole wheat kernels that can be added to bread, cooked as cereal or a side dish, or ground into whole wheat flour.

Wheat bran: The coarse, dark-brown outer layers of the whole wheat kernel. A by-product of white flour, bran is sweet and nutty, adding texture to baked goods.

Wheat germ: Soft, oily part of the wheat kernel, the germ contains the most vitamins and minerals of the kernel. It's no wonder since the germ is really the embryo that grows a new wheat plant. Available both raw and toasted, adds a delicious crunch to lots of foods like breads, salads, vegetables, casseroles, and yogurt.

Zucchini Casserole

When you go to the Vancouver Farmers' Market, you can't miss the Johnson Family Farms booth, it's huge. Over 3 generations grow over a dozen kinds of peppers and hard to find vegetables at the family farm in Yakima Valley. When you shop at the Market, be sure to try out their fresh peppers, roasted right at the Market.

Packed with vegetables, rice, and cheese, this casserole qualifies as a vegetable entree or side dish.

2 large zucchini (about 1 1/2 pounds)
1 cup chopped onion
4 cups chopped plum tomatoes
1/4 cup chopped fresh basil

1/2 teaspoon salt
1/4 teaspoon pepper
1 cup uncooked instant rice
1 1/2 cups shredded sharp cheese, divided

CUT ZUCCHINI lengthwise into 1/8-inch thick slices. Spray a broiler pan with a non-stick spray and arrange zucchini slices in pan. Broil 5 minutes on each side; set aside.

Coat a large skillet with non-stick cooking spray. Sauté onion over medium-high heat for 4 minutes. Add tomatoes, basil, salt and pepper; bring to a boil. Reduce heat and simmer 5 minutes, stirring occasionally. Remove from heat; stir in rice and 1/2 cup cheese.

Arrange half the zucchini slices in bottom of a 2-quart casserole coated with cooking spray. Spoon half of the rice mixture over zucchini. Repeat layers with remaining zucchini slices and rice mixture. Sprinkle with remaining 1 cup cheese. Bake in a preheated 350 degree oven for 20 minutes or until heated through. Serves 6.

JOHNSON FAMILY FARMS

Columbia Gold Barbecue Pizza

You'll love this unique and tasty barbecue style pizza lavished with fresh vegetables, chicken, and cheese.

Use your favorite pizza crust (or Boboli). Spread on Columbia Gold BBQ Sauce and top with grilled teriyaki chicken or cooked beef. Then top with chopped tomatoes, bell peppers, green onions, olives, and mushrooms. Cover with shredded mozzarella and cheddar cheese. Bake at 350 degrees for 15 to 20 minutes.

Gary Carr
COLUMBIA GOLD BBQ SAUCE COMPANY

Salmon Ala Columbia Gold

A winner that's sure to please at any meal.

2 pounds salmon fillets
6 tablespoons Columbia Gold
  Teriyaki Sauce

Juice from 1 orange
1 clove garlic, minced
3 tablespoons brown sugar

MIX TERIYAKI SAUCE, orange and minced garlic, then spoon over salmon. Let sit for 2 to 4 hours, then place fillets on a foil-lined cookie sheet. Sprinkle brown sugar evenly over the fillets. Cook on low heat in covered barbecue for about 20 minutes or until fish is flaking.

Gary Carr
COLUMBIA GOLD BBQ SAUCE COMPANY

---

the garlic difference

What's your preference? Do you want garlic that's easy-to-peel or long on storage? How garlic performs depends in part on which type of garlic you have—hardneck or softneck.

Believed to be the original descendants from wild garlic, the cloves of the hardneck are usually larger. Because its skin isn't as tight, it's also easier to peel. For this same reason hardneck garlic won't store as well, and depending on the quality, that can be anywhere from 1 month to 5 months from when it was harvested.

Softnecks are harder to peel because their skin is tighter, but this is what makes them great for storing. Given the right conditions, they can keep up to a year.

Golden Sunrise Chicken

Barbecued chicken has never been so easy, or so delicious!

1 large oven cooking bag
3 tablespoons flour
1 cup Columbia Gold Barbecue Sauce

1/4 cup orange juice
8 skinless chicken pieces

SHAKE 1 TABLESPOON flour in oven bag. Combine rest of flour, BBQ sauce and juice. Arrange chicken in even layer. Pour sauce over chicken and place in a 13 x 9 x 2-inch baking pan.

Bake at 350 degrees until chicken is tender, about 50 minutes. Remove chicken, stir sauce and spoon over chicken on serving platter. Serves 6 to 8.

Gary Carr
COLUMBIA GOLD BBQ SAUCE COMPANY

Canned Apple Pie Filling

Deliciously convenient for when you want an apple pie fast and quick. Just open your jar of homemade apple pie filling, put in a frozen pie crust, and it's ready to go.

4 1/2 cups sugar	10 cups water
1 cup cornstarch	3 tablespoons lemon juice
1 1/2 teaspoons cinnamon	1 teaspoon salt
1/8 teaspoon nutmeg	5 1/2 pounds apples, sliced

BLEND TOGETHER IN A large pot; sugar, cornstarch, cinnamon, and nutmeg. Stir in water and cook, stirring constantly, until thick and bubbly. Stir in lemon juice and salt.

Pack sliced apples into hot pint jars, leaving a 1-inch head space at top. Fill with hot syrup, removing air bubbles so syrup completely fills jars. Process in a boiling-water canner for 15 minutes. Yields about 5 pint jars.

JOHNSON FAMILY FARMS

Peach Cobbler

This recipe originally came from Louise Logge and it has become one of my favorites. Enjoy with ice cream or cream on top, but it's also fantastic served without.

2 cups sliced peaches	1 cup flour
1 cup sugar	1 cup sugar
6 tablespoons butter or margarine	1 cup milk
(3/4 stick)	2 teaspoons baking powder

This recipe isnt good — far too much sugar & it tastes uncooked — too loose

COMBINE THE PEACHES and 1 cup sugar in a bowl; set aside. Melt butter in a 9 x 9-inch baking dish (microwave is fine). Combine flour, the other 1 cup sugar, milk, and baking powder in a bowl. Mix until it comes out the consistency of pancake batter. Pour batter in the middle of the melted butter; DO NOT STIR. Then pour the peach-sugar combo in the middle of the batter; DO NOT STIR. Bake in a preheated 350 degree oven for 45 minutes. Serves 6.

Amy Blankenship
VANCOUVER FARMERS' MARKET ASSISTANT

Fresh Farm Apple Roly-Poly

Former flower child Carolyn Thurber never left the "whole earth" movement or Clark County, so it seems like the Market is a fitting place for her. Perhaps that's why she spends her time as Market Manager for the Vancouver Market, promoting, marketing, and recruiting for fresh from the earth produce.

This is something like apple pie but easier to make...almost fail-safe...and uses less apples. You can also substitute a peach/rhubarb combination for the apples.

2 3/4 cups all-purpose flour
2 tablespoons sugar
1 tablespoon baking powder
1/4 teaspoon salt
6 tablespoons butter or shortening
1 egg, lightly beaten

3/4 cup milk
2 1/2 to 3 cups peeled and thinly
  sliced fresh farm apples
1 cup sugar
2 teaspoons cinnamon or to taste

BUTTER A 5 X 9-INCH loaf pan. Sift flour, first sugar, baking powder, and salt together in a medium bowl. Cut in butter or shortening until mixture resembles coarse cornmeal. In a separate bowl, add egg and milk; beat well. Add the egg/milk mixture to the dry mixture and stir just to moisten all ingredients.

Turn dough onto a floured board. Knead 4 to 6 times; dough will still be on the dry side. Roll out 1/2-inch thick into a 9 x 11-inch rectangle. Cover dough with apple slices, spread with sugar/cinnamon mixture and press in gently. Starting with the 9-inch side, roll up the dough. Place the roll in the prepared pan.

Bake until the top is golden and the juice is bubbling out the sides, about 50 minutes. Cool for 15 minutes before serving. Slice in the pan and serve with a spatula; this roly-poly is very tender. Serve with ice cream or whipped cream. Drizzle with raspberry sauce or butterscotch sauce. Makes approximately 8 servings.

Carolyn Thurber
VANCOUVER FARMERS' MARKET MANAGER

for a cough or consumption	Just be thankful you didn't live 300 years ago. If you came down with a cough back then, this recipe could be your fate.

"Take 30 garden snails & 30 Earth worms of middling sise, bruise ye snails & wash them and ye worms in fair water, cut ye worms in peices. Boil these in a quart of Spring water to a pint. Pour in boiling hot on 2 ounces of Candied Eringo root sliced thin. When it is cold strain it thro's a flannel bag. Take a quarter of a pint of it warm, with an Equal quantity of Cows' Milk. Continue this course till well."

THE RECEIPT BOOK OF MRS. ANN BLENCOWE, 1694

My Mom's Tomato Soup Cake

Robert and Pamela Keaton of Carworks came up with a neat design for recycling. They make custom three-tiered carts designed to fit the recycling bins. Now you can save energy, that is your own, and wheel the carts right out to the curb.

Spicy cake with tempting tomato flavor that takes you by surprise.

3/4 cup shortening
1 1/4 cups sugar
2 eggs
3 cups flour
1 teaspoon baking powder
1 teaspoon cinnamon
1 teaspoon nutmeg

1 teaspoon cloves
1 can condensed tomato soup
3/4 cup water
1 teaspoon baking soda
3/4 cup raisins
3/4 cup chopped nuts

CREAM TOGETHER the eggs, sugar, and shortening in a large bowl. Add flour, baking powder and spices; stir to combine. In a separate bowl, mix well the tomato soup, water, baking soda, raisins, and nuts. Add to batter; stir to combine.

Pour batter in a prepared loaf or bundt pan. Bake in a preheated 350 degree oven for 45 minutes or until center springs back when lightly touched. Let stand 24 hours before cutting. Makes 1 loaf.

Pamela J. Keaton
CARTWORKS

Peanut Brittle

Mary Palena has been with the Vancouver Farmers' Market since its beginning. Being in her 80's doesn't stop her from cooking up a storm so she can bring her homemade breads, rolls, pies, and fresh herbs to the market.

Fresh always is best, even with homemade peanut brittle.

1 cup sugar
1/2 cup light corn syrup
1/4 cup water
1 cup shelled raw peanuts

1 tablespoon butter
1 1/2 teaspoons baking soda
1/4 teaspoon vanilla

COOK SUGAR, CORN SYRUP, and water until it spins a thread in water test. (Syrup spins 2-inch thread when dropped from spoon in cup of water.) Then add peanuts and butter. Cook until light golden brown, stirring constantly so it won't stick or burn.

Remove from stove and add baking soda and vanilla. Stir rapidly and pour out at once on a heavily greased surface. Let cool; then break into pieces.

Mary Palena
PALENA FARMS

basil storage tips	Unlike other produce, basil should not be stored in the refrigerator. Basil stored this way will usually last only 2 or 3 days and often turns black within the first 24 hours. The only exception would be to spin the leaves dry in a salad spinner after washing. Then place spun-dried leaves in a storage bag that zips, pressing out as much air as possible. If prepared this way, basil stored in the refrigerator can keep up to a week.
	There is an easier way to keep basil fresh once it has been cut. Keep it handy right on the kitchen counter in a glass of water. By changing the water daily, basil can be kept fresh and ready to use for up to two weeks. It's convenient, and the wonderful aroma will continue to freshen and scent your kitchen.

If your plants are being attacked by aphids, those tiny pests that suck the life-giving sap out of your plants, then fight back. Here are a few natural alternatives to try.

Release lacewings or ladybugs to do battle for you. One ladybug larva can devour 40 aphids in just one hour. Up to 60 aphids an hour is the amount consumed by a voracious lacewing larva.

aphid attack

- Plant nectar-filled flowers to encourage the hover fly, also known as the syrphid fly. This small bee-like fly is so named for its ability to "hover" is one spot.

- Try companion planting. Onions, radishes, coriander (cilantro), garlic, petunias, and nasturtiums all help to repel aphids.

- Lay a mulch of aluminum foil to create a reflected light that will confuse flying aphids. They won't know where to land.

- Make a homemade "tea spray" from rhubarb or elderberry leaves. High in oxalic acid, this spray will deter aphids.

Garlic or red pepper sprays also help keep aphids away from prized plants. Check out your local garden center or retail catalog for a spray made from the seeds of the Neem tree. (Bioneem is one such product.)

Mango Jam · Apricot Jalapeño Jelly

Southwest Fiesta Fruit Salsa

Panzanella BreadSalad

Summer Tomato Salad

Nectarine Salad

Delightful Dilled Pasta Salad

French Onion Soup

Willie Green's Winter Squash Soup

Sweet Onion Tart

Herbed Baked Potatoes

Garlic & Basil Pasta

Spiced Pecans · Zucchini Bars

Mini Cheese Cakes

MORE FARMERS' MARKETS

ANACORTES FARMERS' MARKET

LOCATION:

Depot Arts Center; 7th Street & "R" Avenue
Third week of May to mid-October
Saturdays, 9:00 a.m. - 2:00 p.m.

THE ANACORTES FARMERS' MARKET IS LOCATED AT THE OLD TRAIN DEPOT IN TOWN, NOW an art gallery and center for cultural activities. Known for its array of locally grown produce, seafood and tempting treats, the Market also brings in excellent crafters who add to the total shopping experience. Sit down and relax with a game of dominos or checkers under shaded umbrellas.

COWLITZ COMMUNITY FARMERS' MARKET

LOCATION:

Cowlitz County Expo Center, Fairgrounds Parking Lot
April thru October
Tuesdays and Saturdays, 8:00 a.m. - 1:00 p.m.

THE COWLITZ COMMUNITY FARMERS' MARKET WAS STARTED BY THE COMMUNITY ACTION Program as a way for senior citizens to sell excess produce from their community gardens. Since then the Market has grown tremendously and has become the place to go for locally grown fresh berries, fruits and vegetables.

WOODINVILLE FARMERS' MARKET

LOCATION:

13205 NE 175th Street, next to City Hall
April thru October
Saturdays, 9:00 a.m. - 4:00 p.m.

LOCATED IN THE NORTHEAST SECTOR OF KING COUNTY, WOODINVILLE FARMERS' MARKET is a group of food producers and processors, crafters and entertainers of all ages who are committed to providing an innovative, exciting, regional market place. After the Market, enjoy the wineries, bike trails, historic area and beauty representing the richness and diversity of Washington State.

Mango Jam

Colleen Rutten of Colleen's Jams & Jellies sells a complete line of jams, jellies, marmalade, vinegars, mustard, fruit topping and marinades at the Woodinville Farmers' Market.

Mangos cook to form a rich sweet jam. Try it on toast or scones.

4 to 5 medium size ripe mangos	1 box Sure Jel Pectin
Orange juice	4 cups sugar
Juice of 1 lemon	1/8 teaspoon cinnamon

PEEL AND PIT MANGOS. Chop fruit into small chunks and measure. Add enough orange juice to bring to 4 cups. (Add no more than 1/2 cup orange juice.)

Bring a large pot of water to a rolling boil. Add jelly jars and lids; boil for 10 minutes. Leave jars & lids in water until ready to fill.

In a large pot or sauce pan, bring mango/orange juice mixture, lemon juice and box of pectin to a full boil; stir constantly. Boil for 1 to 2 minutes. Reduce heat if mixture boils uncontrollably.

Add sugar and return to a full boil. Boil for 2 minutes and remove from heat. Stir in cinnamon and ladle mixture into hot jelly jars. Wipe threads of jars clean and put on lids. Invert jars for 5 minutes to form a vacuum seal. Fills about 5 jelly jars.

Colleen Rutten
COLLEEN'S JAMS & JELLIES

---

deterents for bad bugs

You can keep many of your favorite plants bug-free with these organic tips:

- Eliminate nearby weeds.

- Grow flowering plants to encourage beneficial insects.

- For slugs and snails; hand-pick, set out beer traps, or use a copper barrier strip around vulnerable plants.

- Keep cabbage worms and loopers in check by releasing trichogramma wasps or dusting plants with BT (Bacillus thuringiensis).

- Mulch plants with catnip to repel flea beetles.

- Leafhoppers will hop away when petunias or geraniums are nearby. Better yet, surround your garden with birdhouses. Swallows love leafhopper nymphs (as well as other pest insects).

- Keep aphids and leafhoppers off plants with a strong jet spray from the garden hose. For a serious pest problem, dust plants with diatomaceous earth, spray with Neem (Bioneem for instance), or keep bugs off altogether by protecting plants from the start with a floating row cover.

Apricot Jalapeño Jelly

This is a sweet yet subtly hot jelly that's great on bagels, cold meat, crackers and cream cheese.

1 cup chopped apricots*
1 1/2 cups vinegar
1 12-ounce jar pickled jalapenos, drained

6 cups sugar
1 box Sure Gel Pectin

* reconstituted dried apricots add a more intense flavor than fresh, but use whatever is available.

BRING A LARGE POT of water to a rolling boil. Add jelly jars and lids; boil for 10 minutes. Leave in water until ready to fill.

In a large pan, add apricots, vinegar, jalapenos, and sugar. Bring to a full boil over high heat, stirring constantly. Boil for 2 minutes. Add pectin and boil for 2 minutes more. Remove from heat.

Ladle mixture into hot jelly jars. Wipe threads of jars clean and put on lids. Invert jars to form a vacuum seal. Jalapenos will float to the surface, so if you invert the jars several times during cooling, the jalapenos will be evenly distributed in the jelly.

Colleen Rutten
COLLEEN'S JAMS & JELLIES

Southwest Fiesta Fruit Salsa

When Gloria Shelton's job was downsized more than 5 years ago, she became intensely aware of the high prices for herbs and spices in the store. So she set out to provide quality herb/spice products at a reasonable price. The result is her company, Burrows Bay Herbs & Spices. Now she sells custom herb and spice blends, mustard mixes, herbal brews, mulling spices, teas, and giant "bath" tea bags at the Anacortes Farmers' Market.

Serve with grilled chicken or pork, or as a dip with tortilla chips. For a healthy alternative, use thin slices of jicama to dip the salsa. Enjoy!

2 cups coarsely chopped ripe fruit; mango, papaya, peaches, nectarines or a combination

2 kiwi fruit, peeled and coarsely chopped

1 bunch green onions, white and some green parts, coarsely chopped

1 red pepper, seeded and coarsely chopped

Juice of 1 lime

1 tablespoon (or more to taste) Southwest Fiesta Blend*

1/4 cup snipped fresh cilantro

* *Available thru Burrows Bay Herbs & Spices at the Anacortes Farmers' Market.*

MIX ALL INGREDIENTS in a non-metallic bowl; cover and place in the refrigerator. Allow the flavors to blend for at least an hour. Yields 2 1/2 to 3 cups.

Gloria K. Shelton
BURROWS BAY HERBS & SPICES

Panzanella Breadsalad

A summer specialty featuring an exceptional mingling of basil and sun-ripened tomatoes.

1 pound stale country style bread, about four 1-inch thick slices

4 ripe tomatoes, quartered

1 medium red onion, finely sliced

1 cucumber, peeled and diced in big chunks

1 bunch fresh basil, coarsely chopped or torn

1/2 cup extra virgin olive oil

3 tablespoons aged red wine vinegar

Salt and freshly ground black pepper to taste

SOFTEN THE BREAD SLICES in a bowl of cool water, then squeeze each slice gently to rid of excess liquid. Tear the bread into chunks, discarding the thick crusts. Drop into salad bowl and add the tomatoes, onion, cucumber, and basil. Toss to mix.

Mix together the oil, vinegar, salt and pepper for a dressing. Pour dressing over salad and toss well to coat. Serve chilled.

Sous Chef Andrew Norby
THE SOUTHPARK GRILL
PORTLAND, OREGON

lots of lettuce	Variety	Description
	Loose Leaf	
	Brunia	Red-tinged oak leaves, sweet flavor and slow to bolt
	Red Fire	Deep red leaves, sweet & bolt-resistant
	Red Sails	Bronze-red, very popular, and most bolt-resistant in our trials
	Simpson's Elite	Bright green, tender and slow bolting
	Two Star	Dark green, less frilly than most. A good early lettuce
	Butterhead	
	Buttercrunch	Juicy, rich flavor. Popular green variety
	Merveille 4 Saison	Ruby red with green hearts, very tender
	Optima	Dark green Boston type, reliable good-tasting variety
	Romaine	
	Cimmaron	Bronze-red color; tall, tender, and slow bolting
	Kalura	Strong heat-tolerance; big and thick light green leaves
	Majestic Red	Deep burgundy red, crisp and loose head
	Plato II	Slightly savoyed, medium green meaty leaves
	Crisphead	
	Ithaca	Resists tip burn; popular green head lettuce
	Salinas	Resists heat or chill; big solid heads
	Summertime	Medium size, heat tolerant. Great variety
	French Crisp	
	Nevada	Bright green, extra crisp with great flavor
	Sierra	Red-tinged leaves very crisp & sweet. A Camelot favorite.

Summer Tomato Salad

Brighten your salad with a colorful mix of red, orange, yellow, and pink tomatoes. This makes a nice salad for one.

1/2 pound assorted fresh tomatoes, sliced
1 teaspoon capers
1 teaspoon chopped fresh oregano
1 tablespoon goat cheese

1 tablespoon Tuscan red wine vinegar
1 tablespoon extra virgin olive oil
Salt and freshly ground black pepper
  to taste

ARRANGE TOMATO SLICES on serving plate and top with rest of ingredients.

Sous Chef Andrew Norby
THE SOUTHPARK GRILL
PORTLAND, OREGON

deer proofing lessons

Deer are browsers, but they'll often leave less desirable plants alone when their favorites are at hand. A lilac bush in a garden of roses will usually remain untouched. In a garden lacking their favorite foods, lilac probably will be the main course.

One way to deerproof your garden is to grow plants you're willing to sacrifice to protect your favorites. Another is to surround your favorites with plants deer hate, or simply limit your garden to herbaceous perennials that tend to make deer do an about-face.

Different species of deer tend to have different favorites. Ever the connoisseurs, they might devour young plants but avoid an older specimen of the same variety. As the deer population increases—a function of fewer natural predators and more suburban development—there's naturally less food to go around. When dry conditions make food even more scarce, deer may nibble on plants they normally might leave alone.

The only 100% sure-proof way to keep deer from munching on your flowers is to deer-fence the area you want to protect with an 8-foot tall fence. If you don't want your fence that conspicuous in the landscape, try two 4-foot tall fences spaced 3-feet apart. Deer can jump high and they can jump wide, but they usually can't do both at the same time. Here are a few other remedies that may help keep deer damage under control.

- Hang strong-smelling deodorant soap bars like Dial or Zest in trees or on stakes around the perimeter of beds.

- The smell of other animals often is enough to turn deer away. If you don't have pets, use dog, cat, or human hair as mulch for susceptible plants. Blood meal and fish emulsion can deter deer, as can fox urine (available at hunting departments in sporting good stores).

- Hang pie pans around the garden so they make noise when the wind blows, or install an outside motion-detector light. One gardener keeps her roses safe with blinking outdoor miniature Christmas lights.

- Try commercial deer repellents, available at gardening centers. Look for egg-based products.

- Protect a beloved specimen with a cage of chicken wire.

- When all else fails, garden in hanging baskets.

Nectarine Salad

A medley of nectarines, fennel, and balsamic vinegar for exceptional taste.

4 nectarines, sliced
1 fennel bulb, cut julienne style
   then sautéed
1/2 tablespoon chopped bronze fennel

1 teaspoon cracked black pepper
1 tablespoon balsamic vinegar
1 tablespoon lemon oil*

* Or substitute 1 teaspoon lemon juice with enough oil to make 1 tablespoon.

PLACE ALL INGREDIENTS in a bowl and toss. Keep refrigerated until ready to serve.

Sous Chef Tim Pipes
N.W. FUSION

---

spinach flavor cousins	With its subtly rich flavor and buttery texture, spinach is a cut above other greens. But as soon as the weather turns warm, spinach is ready to call it quits and suddenly takes to bolting. Spinach just can't stand the heat and that's bad news for those who love the great taste of spinach. There's good new though. When the heat is on, that mellow flavor and smooth texture can still be yours by growing these flavorful cousins.

Garden Orach has arrowhead-leaves with a texture and taste similar to spinach. This old-time pot herb is also known as "mountain spinach", and grows from 2 to 5 feet in height. Leaves can be gold, green, or purplish-red depending on the variety grown. This hardy annual is tolerant to both frost and heat. Use the young tender leaves for sautéing and tossing in salads. The older leaves are best cooked, especially in soups and stews.

New Zealand Spinach is a summer-time spinach substitute that succeeds in the heat when others fail. The lime green pointed leaves resemble spinach in appearance, and are best when cooked or frozen for later use. Grows up to 2 feet tall.

Swiss Chard is actually a close relative of beets, but it's very similar in taste to spinach with perhaps more of a buttery texture. The red varieties are more pronounced in flavor while the green varieties are slightly more tender and mild in taste. Moderately winter hardy, Swiss chard will also tolerate more heat than spinach ever could. Use young leaves fresh in salads, or cook slightly by steaming or sautéing. Older leaves are best cooked in soups and stews.

Delightful Dilled Pasta Salad

Dill delight is a blend of sesame, dill and celery seed; chives, parsley, and dill weed plus cracked black pepper, onion and garlic granules.

8 ounces pasta, cooked according to package directions (orzo is particularly good).

4 to 6 ounces smoked salmon, cut into 1/4-inch pieces*

1 10-ounce package tiny peas, cooked

1/2 cup mayonnaise

1/2 cup sour cream

2 tablespoons Dill Delight**

* *Or substitute 6 ounces tuna, drained and flaked.*
** *Available thru Burrows Bay Herbs & Spices at the Anacortes Farmers' Market.*

MIX COOKED PASTA, salmon, and peas in a large bowl. In a smaller bowl, blend together the mayonnaise, sour cream, and Dill Delight to make the dressing. You may adjust the proportions to taste. Add dressing to pasta mix and blend thoroughly. Chill and serve cold.

This recipe is very flexible and can be made with cooked chicken or turkey. You can add diced onion or scallions to taste. Serves 4.

Gloria K. Shelton
BURROWS BAY HERBS & SPICES

MORE FARMERS' MARKETS

French Onion Soup

A classic French soup guaranteed to bring rave reviews.

1 stick butter
2 pounds onions, cut julienne style
1 tablespoon diced fresh garlic
1 cup white wine
1 cup brandy
8 cups fresh chicken stock

2 bay leaves
Salt and freshly ground black
   pepper to taste
8 round croutons
1 pound grated cheese (use a combination
   of Swiss, Parmesan & Gruyere cheese)

CARAMELIZE ONIONS and garlic in butter. Deglaze the pan with wine and reduce. Add brandy and reduce. Add bay leaves and chicken stock, then simmer. Season with salt and pepper. Ladle soup into four terrines. Place two croutons on top and sprinkle with cheese blend. Place under a broiler until golden brown and bubbly. Serves 4.

Executive Sous Chef Andrew Nordby
THE HEATHMAN RESTAURANT
PORTLAND, OREGON

---

cooking with herbs

Here are a few cooking tips when using herbs and spices.

- Dried herbs are more concentrated in flavor than fresh, so use two to three times more fresh herb to equal the amount used for dried.

- For best flavor, leave herbs and spices whole until ready to use.

- When ready to use, chop leaves finely so more cut surface is exposed, releasing more herbal flavor.

- Scissors are a great utensil for mincing fresh herbs.

- The flavor of herbs is lost with extended cooking. Add herbs to soups and stews about 45 minutes before it's ready. Delicate fresh herbs like French tarragon, basil, and chervil should be added within the last 5 minutes of cooking.

- Be conservative until you're familiar with the flavor and strength of the herb being used. Remember, you can always add more later.

Willie Green's Winter Squash Soup

A unique heirloom pumpkin from France, rouge d'etampes is known in America as Cinderella pumpkin. Flavor is fantastic in pies and especially soup.

1 10 point rouge d'etampes squash
4 delicata squash
2 to 3 tablespoons brown sugar
2 tablespoon butter
4 ounces salt pork
1 large onion, finely diced

4 garlic cloves, chopped fine
3 to 4 quarts chicken stock
1 red bell pepper, chopped
12 ounces half and half
Salt and pepper to taste

CUT ROUGE INTO manageable pieces and delicata in half lengthwise. Scoop out seed and place flesh side up in baking pans. Sprinkle a little brown sugar and place pat of butter onto each piece. Add a little water to each pan, cover with foil, and bake at 450 degrees until squash is fork-tender, about 45 to 50 minutes. When cool, scoop out cooked flesh and set aside.

Remove rind from salt pork and cut into 1/2-inch pieces. Chop finely in a food processor. In a large saucepan, render salt pork over medium heat, add onions and garlic, and then cook until onions are tender. Add winter squash flesh, red pepper and chicken stock. Stir to mix and simmer about an hour. Remove from heat, and when cooled down, puree in food processor till smooth. Pour soup into saucepan and return to simmer. Add half and half, season with salt and pepper to taste, and then serve. Makes 6 to 10 servings.

Jeff Miller
WILLIE GREEN'S ORGANIC FARM
MONROE, WASHINGTON

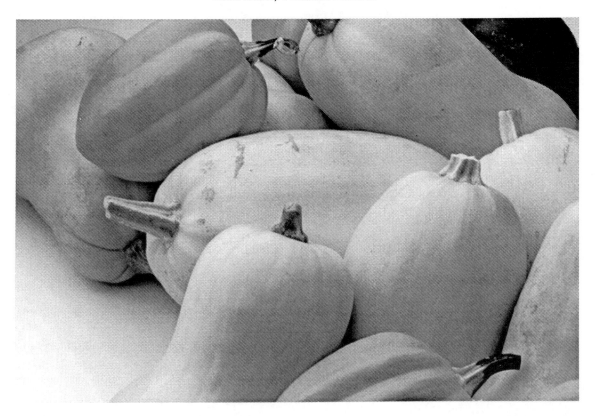

Sweet Onion Tart

Look for sweet Walla Walla onions beginning in June. Excellent choice for this tart.

3 bunches sweet onions (about 8 medium)	1 pint non-fat sour cream
2 bunches scallions	2 eggs
1 tablespoon olive oil	1 9-inch pie crust, lightly baked
1 tablespoon Burrows Bay dried herbs*	but not browned

* Available thru Burrows Bay Herbs & Spices at the Anacortes Farmers' Market. Thyme is especially good with the onions but you can also try Greek Isle, Italian Herbs, Pizza Herbs, Herb Medley, or Dill Delight.

WASH AND TRIM scallions and onions; slice them all thinly to make about 6 cups. Heat the oil in a large frying pan and sauté the onions over medium heat, stirring frequently so they don't brown; they should be limp and translucent. During the last minute of cooking, add the dried herbs.

In a bowl, beat together sour cream and eggs. After turning off the heat under the onions, add the sour cream mixture, stirring thoroughly. Don't cook, just let the pan warm it up. Add this filling to the pie crust and bake in a preheated oven at 375 degrees for 45 minutes or until a knife inserted in the middle comes out clean. Serve warm. Makes 4 to 6 servings, depending on who's doing the serving!

Gloria K. Shelton
BURROWS BAY HERBS & SPICES

---

the great tomato debate

As President, Ronald Reagan stated that catsup served in school lunchroom cafeterias met the required serving for a vegetable. However, botanically speaking, the tomato is actually a fruit, or more specifically, a berry.

Whether the tomato is a fruit or a vegetable is a debate that began back in 1883 with the Tariff Act which allowed the duty-free importation of fruits, but not vegetables. Three years later an importer named John Nix protested when a customs agent levied a duty on his imported tomatoes, even though Nix knew they were botanically fruits.

This controversy went all the way to the Supreme Court and in 1893 Justice Horace Gray ruled the tomato a vegetable: "Botanically speaking, tomatoes are the fruit of the vine, just as are cucumbers, squashes, beans and peas. But in the common language of the people...all these vegetables...are usually served at dinner...and not, like fruits, generally as dessert." So by law from that day forward the tomato became a vegetable.

Herbed Baked Potatoes

Delicious red potatoes gently roasted to flavorful perfection.

3 pounds red potatoes, cut into 1-inch pieces
1 tablespoon olive oil
2 tablespoons Herb Medley

SPRAY A GLASS 8 x 11-inch baking dish with a cooking spray and put the potatoes in. Drizzle olive oil over the potatoes and toss them to coat with oil. Sprinkle herbs over the potatoes and toss to distribute.

Bake potatoes in a preheated 375 degree oven for 1 hour, tossing the potatoes every 15 minutes. They will be crispy-tender when done. Leftovers, if there are any, are delicious reheated for breakfast.

Gloria K. Shelton
BURROWS BAY HERBS & SPICES

a pound of this, a pound of that	Take a pound each of butter, sugar, eggs, and flour, and what do you come up with? Pound cake of course, and that's how it got its name. Back in the colonial days, it also took a pound of energy to hand beat the batter till it was ready.

Garlic and Basil Pasta

Having grown up on farms, Dixie and Scott Edwards now grow all sorts of vegetables of their own like garlic, sugar snap peas, and potatoes for the Cowlitz Community Farmers' Market. That is when they're not growing native plants for stream and wetland restoration through their business, Watershed Garden Works.

Fresh from the garden flavor for a pasta you'll want to make again and again.

1/3 cup whole garlic cloves, chopped
1/3 cup olive oil
2 to 3 heads broccoli, chopped and
   lightly steamed (or use raw)

2 to 3 cups spiral pasta, cooked and drained
1/2 cup chopped fresh basil
1/3 cup parmesan cheese

HEAT OIL IN A LARGE saucepan; stir garlic and cook until soft. Combine remaining ingredients and toss lightly to coat. Serves 6.

Dixie Edwards
WATERSHED GARDENWORKS

---

care for a pear?

European pears are picked when mature but not yet ripe since they don't ripen well on the tree. Usually pears you buy will still be firm and unripe. To ripen pears, let stand at room temperature (although some varieties do best when ripened in cold storage) until a gentle thumb pressure applied to the base of the stem yields slightly. Now your pear is ripe with juicy sweet flavor and ready to eat, or store in the refrigerator for later. In a hurry to ripen those pears? Place them in a single layer in a paper bag and fold over the top.

Anjou—A Northwest favorite that's abundant with sweet juicy flavor. Yellow and dark red-skinned varieties available.

Bartlett—Thin skinned, very sweet and tender. Ripens to a bright yellow or slightly blushed, also a bright red variety. Excellent for fresh eating and canning. Red variety especially stunning in fresh salads and fruit desserts.

Bosc—Firm fleshed and flavorful with brownish skin and crunchy texture. Very sweet and juicy flavor is excellent for baking, poaching, grilling, fresh eating, and salads. Tastes best after storing a month or two.

Bennett—Large yellow-green pear with red blush resembling Bartlett in size. Excellent tasting fresh or dehydrated.

Comice—Large yellow pear with melting flesh. One of the sweetest and juiciest of pears. Best flavor comes after storing a month at room temperature.

Orcas—Discovered on Orcas Island in Washington, it has now become a regional favorite. Very attractive large, flavorful yellow fruit with ruby blush. Juicy flavor and buttery flesh are great for canning, drying, or eating fresh.

Rescue—With its huge beautiful fruit and sweet, smooth and juicy flesh, Rescue is quite an attention getter. Yellow fruit with bright red-orange blush.

Seckel—Known as the "sugar pear" for its very sweet extraordinary flavor. Reddish blushed yellow fruits are sweet as candy when dried. Ideal as a dessert pear and for canning.

Spiced Pecans

Sensational nutty flavor delicately spiced with cinnamon, nutmeg, allspice, and cloves.

1 egg white
2 tablespoon vanilla
3/4 cup brown sugar
1/4 teaspoon salt

2 tablespoons cinnamon
1/2 teaspoon each nutmeg, allspice,
  and cloves
1 pound pecans

WHISK EGG WHITE until frothy, then whisk in vanilla. In a separate bowl, whisk together sugar, salt, and spices. Fold nuts into egg whites, then stir in spice mixture.

Spread onto parchment lined sheet pans and bake, stirring often, at 300 degrees for 10 to 15 minutes or until nuts feel dry. Cool and store in airtight container.

Sous Chef Charles Flint
HUDSON'S BAR & GRILL
VANCOUVER, WASHINGTON

Zucchini Bars

Having been dairy farmers for over 35 years, Roberta and Jerry Peterson have now retired, if you can call it that. Peterson Farms grows an assortment of berries, plants, and all types of produce which Roberta takes to the Cowlitz Community Farmers' Market.

I have never served this without guests wanting the recipe.

3 eggs
1 cup oil
2 cups sugar
2 cups grated zucchini
3 teaspoons vanilla
2 cups flour
1 teaspoon salt

1/4 teaspoon baking powder
2 teaspoons baking soda
1/2 cup soft butter
1 8-ounce package cream cheese
3 1/2 cups powdered sugar
2 teaspoons vanilla

IN A MIXER OR by hand, whisk together eggs, oil, sugar, zucchini, and 3 teaspoons vanilla. In a separate bowl, combine flour, salt, baking powder and soda. Add flour mixture to zucchini mixture and stir just until combined; do not overmix.

In a small bowl add butter, cream cheese, powdered sugar, and vanilla; beat until smooth and creamy. Set aside to use as cream cheese frosting.

Pour zucchini batter in a greased 12 x 16-inch jelly roll pan and bake in a preheated 350 degree oven for 30 minutes or until brown. When cool, frost with cream cheese frosting.

Roberta Peterson
PETERSON FARMS

Mini Cheese Cakes

Pat and Gerald Biggers of Biggers Berries have been raising 2 acres of raspberries since 1980. They sell their raspberries along with homemade jams, jellies, and pies plus nursery stock and garden produce at the Selah Farmers' Market.

When you just got to satisfy that undeniable sweet hunger, these mini cheesecakes are simply easy to make, very quick, and ohh soo wonderfully tasty.

12 vanilla wafers
2 8-ounce packages cream cheese
1/2 cup sugar

1 teaspoon vanilla
2 eggs

LINE MUFFIN TIN with foil liners. Place one vanilla wafer in each liner. Mix cream cheese, sugar, and vanilla on medium speed until well blended. Add eggs and mix well. Pour over wafers, filling about 3/4 full.

Bake at 325 degrees for 25 minutes. Remove from tin when cool. Chill and top with fruit, preserves, nuts, or chocolate. Makes 12 mini cheese cakes.

Pat Biggers
BIGGERS BERRIES

the lowdown on potatoes	Wouldn't you love to enjoy a deliciously satisfying food that's has no fat and is low in calories? Just reach for a potato. One medium potato contains the following:
	• about 110 calories
	• 23 grams of complex carbohydrate (good for you energy)
	• no fat
	• plenty of potassium and vitamin C

Farmers Markets in Washington

ANACORTES

ANACORTES FARMERS MARKET

Location: 7th Street & R Avenue
May 13 to October 14
Saturdays, 9:00 a.m. - 2:00 p.m.

Contact: Gloria Shelton
1803 Piper Circle
Anacortes, WA 98221
360-293-9404

BAINBRIDGE ISLAND

BAINBRIDGE ISLAND FARMERS MARKET

Location: Madison Avenue & Winslow Way
April 8 to mid October
Saturdays, 9:00 a.m. - 1:00 p.m.

Contact: Jaci Douglas
PO Box 10225
Bainbridge Island, WA 98110
206-855-1500
www.bainbridge.net/farmersmarket

BELFAIR

BELFAIR FARMERS MARKET

Location: Belfair School Playshed (across
from Theler Community Center)
May 6 to October 28
Saturdays, 9:00 a.m. - 3:00 p.m.

Contact: Norma Stencil
PO Box 1649
Belfair, WA 98528
(360) 275-0616

BELLINGHAM

BELLINGHAM FARMERS MARKET ASSN.

Location: Railroad & Chestnut
April 8 to October
Saturdays, 10:00 a.m. - 3:00 p.m.

Contact: Emily Weaver
1101 N. State Street, Suite 104
Bellingham, WA 98225
360-647-2060
www.bellinghamfarmers.org

BELLINGHAM FARMERS MARKET—FAIRHAVEN

Location: 10th & Mills Street
June to September
Wednesdays, 3:00 p.m. - 7:00 p.m.

Contact: Heather Bansmer
PO Box 4083
Bellingham, WA 98227
360-738-1574

BOTHELL

COUNTRY VILLAGE FARMERS MARKET

Location: 238th & Bothell-Everett Hwy. (SR 527)
June 4 to October 8
Fridays, 10:00 a.m. - 3:00 p.m.

Contact: Kaye Hagenberger
LeeannTesorier
PO Box 82660
Kenmore, WA 98028-0660
425-483-2250
www.countryvillagebothell.com

BRIDGEPORT

BRIDGEPORT FARMERS MARKET

Location: Quickie Mart Parking Lot
(Junction Hwy 17 & 173)
June 23 to October 13
Fridays, 9:00 a.m. - Noon

Contact: Verla Groenveld
2365 Tacoma
Bridgeport, WA 98813
509-686-3875

BURLINGTON

BURLINGTON FARMERS MARKET

Location: 600 E. Victoria at Cherry
May to Labor Day
Fridays, 3:00 a.m. - 7:00 p.m.

Contact: Margaret Fleek
901 E. Fairhaven Avenue
Burlington, WA 98233
360-755-9717

CATHLAMET

FARMERS MARKET OF WAHKIAKUM COUNTY

Location: Ocean Beach Hwy. (Hwy. 4) &
Jacobson Road across from
Mace's Drive-In
May 13 to October 21
Saturdays, 10:00 a.m. - 1:00 p.m.

Contact: Jerry Ledtke
68-3 Peterson Road
Skamokawa, WA 98647
360-795-3434

CENTRALIA

LEWIS COUNTY FARMERS MARKET

Location: Pine Street between Tower &
Depot Road
April 14 to October 15
Fridays & Saturdays,
8:00 a.m. - 5:00 p.m.

Contact: Rita Larson
PO Box 272
Chehalis, WA 98532
360-262-3334

CHELAN

CHELAN VALLEY FARMERS MARKET

Location: Johnson Street & Columbia (next to
Chamber of Commerce)
June 3 to October 21
Saturdays, 8:30 a.m. - Noon

Contact: Judy Breznia
PO Box 1954
Chelan, WA 98816
509-682-3243

COLVILLE

COLVILLE FARMERS MARKET

Location: Public Works Parking Lot (corner of
Hawthorne & Elm streets)
April 26 to October 25, August 5
Wednesdays, Noon - 6:00 p.m.

Contact: Pam & Tom Harrison
1133-A Aladdin Rt.
Colville, WA 99114
509-675-1133

NORTHEAST WASHINGTON FARMERS MARKET

Location: Astor & Main
May 6 to October 28
Saturdays, 8:30 a.m. - 1:00 p.m.

Contact: Carol Rolf
PO Box 307
Colville, WA 99114
509-684-2326

COUPEVILLE

COUPEVILLE FARMERS MARKET

Location: 8th & Main
April 1 to October 14
Saturdays, 10:00 a.m. - 2:00 p.m.

Contact: Irene Thomas
PO Box 215
Coupeville, WA 98239
360-678-6757

DAYTON

DAYTON FARMERS MARKET

Location: 5th & Main Street
June 11 to October 29
Sundays, Noon - 4:00 p.m.
Thursdays, 4:00 p.m. - 8:00 p.m.

Contact: Karen Johnson
Patit Creek Farm
321 E. Patit Street
Dayton, WA 99328
509-382-9533

DEER PARK

DEER PARK FARMERS MARKET

Location: Deer Park Fairgrounds on Main Street
May 6 to mid September
Saturdays, 9:00 a.m. - Noon

Contact: Debra Lampe
PO Box 1734
Deer Park, WA 99006
509-276-7766

EDMONDS

EDMONDS MUSEUM SUMMER MARKET

Location: Bell Street, between 5th & 6th
July to September
Saturdays, 9:00 a.m. - 3:00 p.m.

Contact: Bette Bell
PO Box 952
Edmonds, WA 98020
425-775-5650

ELLENSBURG

KITTITAS COUNTY FARMERS MARKET

Location: 5th & Anderson
May 6 to October 28
Saturdays, 9:00 a.m. - 1:00 p.m.

Contact: Katie Patterson
110 W. 6th, Box 242
Ellensburg, WA 98926
509-925-5767

ENUMCLAW

ENUMCLAW COUNTRY MARKET

Location: Griffin & Railroad
April 28 to October 28
Saturdays, 9:30 a.m. - 3:00 p.m.

Contact: Wade Bennett
PO Box 871
Enumclaw, WA 98022
253-825-1962

EVERETT

EVERETT FARMERS MARKET

Location: Everett Marina at Port Gardner
Landing
June 4 to September24
Sundays, 11:00 a.m. - 4:00 p.m.

Contact: Marie Brayman
PO Box 631
Everett, WA 98206
425-347-2790

FORKS

FORKS FARMERS MARKET

Location: Thriftway Parking Lot, Hwy. 101
May 12 to October 15, & April 29
Fridays & Saturdays, 10:00 a.m. -
2:00 p.m.

Contact: Joanne McReynolds
21 Bunker Rd.
Forks, WA 98331
360-374-6623

FRIDAY HARBOR

SAN JUAN FARMERS MARKET

Location: County Courthouse Parking Lot
May 27 to October 27
Saturdays, 10:00 a.m. - 1:00 p.m.

Contact: Tori Zehner
PO Box 3161
Friday harbor, WA 98250
360-378-6301

GIG HARBOR

GIG HARBOR FARMERS MARKET

Location: 3500 Hunt Street N.W. at Hwy. 16
May 6 to October 14
Saturdays, 8:30 a.m. - 2:00 p.m.

Contact: Janice Piercy
PO Box 1014
Wauna, WA 98395
253-884-2496

MINTER CREEK FARMERS MARKET

Location: 118th Street N.W. & SR 302
at Ravensara
June 11 to September 24
Sundays, Noon - 4:00 p.m.

Contact: Janice Piercy
PO Box 1014
Wauna, WA 98395
253-884-2496

GREENBANK

GREENBANK FARMERS MARKET

Location: Greenbank Farm, just off SR 525
May 14 to mid October
Sundays, 11:00 a.m. - 2:00 p.m.

Contact: Ginny Snyder
PO Box 937
Freeland, WA 98249
360-321-5287

HOQUIAM

GRAY'S HARBOR FARMERS MARKET

Location: 1958 Riverside Drive, Hwy. 101
at 20th Street
Year Round
Wednesday to Saturday,
9:00 a.m. - 6:00 p.m.

Contact: Erik Erlander
PO Box 228
Aberdeen, WA 98520
360-538-9747

ISSAQUAH

ISSAQUAH PUBLIC MARKET

Location: 56th Street S.E. & 10th S.E.
April 22 to November 17
Saturdays, 9:00 a.m. - 3:00 p.m.
Sundays, 10:00 a.m. - 2:00 p.m.

Contact: David Sao
PO Box 1307
Issaquah, WA 98027
425-837-3311

KINGSTON

KINGSTON FARMERS MARKET

Location: Kingston Marina at Washington &
Central
May 6 to October 7
Saturdays, 9:00 a.m. - 2:00 p.m.

Contact: Clint Dudley
PO Box 124
Kingston, WA 98346
360-297-7683
www.thenickoftime.com/KFM

KITSAP PENINSULA

PENINSULA FARMERS MARKET

Location: Kitsa County Fairgrounds
Parking Lot
April to September
Tuesdays, 9:00 a.m. - 3:00 p.m.

Contact: Monica Phillips
13687 NW Coho Run
Bremerton, WA 98312
360-830-9502

LAKEBAY

KEY PENINSULA FARMERS MARKET

Location: Volunteer Park at 5514 Key Peninsula
Hwy.
May 12 to September 15
Wednesdays, Noon - 6:00 p.m.

Contact: Janice Piercy
PO Box 1014
Wauna, WA 98395
253-884-2496

LAKEWOOD

LAKEWOOD FARMERS MARKET

Location: Lakewood Mall Parking Lot,
Lakewood Drive
May 4 to September 14
Tuesdays, Noon - 6:00 p.m.

Contact: Janice Piercy
PO Box 1014
Wauna, WA 98395
253-884-2496

LANGLEY

SOUTH WHIDBEY TILTH
FARMERS MARKET

Location: Hwy. 525 at Thompson Road, ½ mile
west of Whidbey Telephone Co.
May 13 to October 28
Saturdays, 10:00 a.m. - 1:00 p.m.

Contact: Caroline Thibodaux
PO Box 252
Langley, WA 98260
360-331-3704

BAYVIEW FARMERS MARKET

Location: Bayview Road (next to Bayview
Farm & Garden)
May 13 to October 28
Saturdays, 10:00 a.m. - 2:00 p.m.

Contact: Debbie Torget
3309 S. East Harbor Road
Langley, WA 98260
360-730-7013

LEAVENWORTH

WENATCHEE VALLEY FARMERS MARKET

Location: Next to City Pool
June to September
Tuesdays, 8:00 a.m. - Noon

Contact: Valerie Schooler
PO Box 2824
Wenatchee, WA 98807
509-667-1343

LONGVIEW

COWLITZ COUNTY COMMUNITY
FARMERS MARKET

Location: Cowlitz County Expo Center,
7th & Washington
May 2 to October 31
Tuesdays & Saturdays, 8:00 a.m. -
1:00 p.m., Saturday only in April

Contact: Terrence Miracle
3296 Nebraska Street
Longview, WA 98632-4275
360-425-1297
www.commercemp.com/home/
cowlitzmarket

MOSES LAKE

COLUMBIA BASIN FARMERS MARKET

Location: Civic Center Park
June 12 to October 23
Saturdays, 7:30 a.m. - 1:00 p.m.

Contact: Bertha Wydler
PO Box 691
Moses Lake, WA 98837
509-787-1305

MOUNT VERNON

SKAGIT VALLEY FARMERS MARKET

Location: The Revetment on the River,
Kincaid Street & Main
June 3 to September 30
Saturdays, 9:00 a.m. - 1:00 p.m.

Contact: Debbie Clough
202 N. 8th
Mount Vernon, WA 98273
360-336-5007

NEWPORT

PEND OREILLE VALLEY EARTH MARKET

Location: Hwy. 2 & 4th at Washington Avenue
May 6 to October 28
Saturdays, 9:00 a.m. - 1:00 p.m.

Contact: Robert Karr
205 N. Craig Avenue
Newport, WA 99156
509-447-2552

NORTH BEND

NORTH BEND FARMERS MARKET

Location: North Bend Senior Center (Main &
Park at SR 202)
June 3 to October 7
Saturdays, 9:00 a.m. - 1:00 p.m.

Contact: Karen Lee
PO Box 1140
North Bend, WA 98045
425-831-5840

OAK HARBOR

OAK HARBOR PUBLIC MARKET

Location: North Whidbey Middle School,
Hwy. 20 (in field next to
chamber office)
June 1 to September 28
Thursdays, 4:00 p.m. - 7:00 p.m.

Contact: Sheila Case-Smith
98 Case Road
Oak Harbor, WA 98277
360-675-0472

OKANOGAN

OKANOGAN VALLEY FARMERS MARKET

Location: American Legion Park (2nd & Harley streets)
May 6 to October 28
Tuesdays, 4:00 p.m. - 7:00 p.m.
Saturdays, 9:00 a.m. - Noon

Contact: Stephanie Clark
PO Box 3181
Omak, WA 98841
509-826-1259

OLYMPIA

OLYMPIA FARMERS MARKET

Location: 700 N. Capitol Way
April to October
Thursdays - Sundays, 10:00 a.m. - 3:00 p.m.
November to December
Saturdays & Sundays, 10:00 a.m. - 3:00 p.m.

Contact: Kevin Corbin
PO Box 7094
Olympia, WA 98507
360-352-9096

OTHELLO

OTHELLO FARMERS MARKET

Location: Pioneer Park (4th & Main)
May 20 to October 28
Saturdays, 7:00 a.m. - Noon

Contact: Nyla Chriswell
755 N. 7th
Othello, WA 99344
509-488-2730

PORT ANGELES

PORT ANGELES FARMERS MARKET

Location: 8th & Chase streets
July to March
Saturdays, 9:00 a.m. - 4:00 p.m.

Contact: Nash Huber
1865 E. Anderson Road
Sequim, WA 98382
360-683-4642

PORT LUDLOW

PORT LUDLOW FARMERS MARKET

Location: Village Center, Oak Bay Road & Paradise Bay Road
April 16 to September 27
Fridays, 9:00 a.m. - 2:00 p.m.

Contact: Don Cooper
PO Box 65070
Port Ludlow, WA 98365-0070
360-437-2300

PORT ORCHARD

PORT ORCHARD FARMERS MARKET

Location: On Waterfront at Bethel & Harris behind Peninsula Feed Store
April 29 to October 28
Saturdays, 9:00 a.m. - 3:00 p.m.

Contact: Carmen Davis
PO Box 8247
Port Orchard, WA 98366
253-857-2657
www.pofarmersmarket.com

PORT TOWNSEND

JEFFERSON COUNTY FARMERS MARKET

Location: City Lot at Madison & Washington
May 6 to October 28
Saturdays, 8:30 a.m. - 1:00 p.m.

Location: Lawrence Street (between Tyler & Polk)
May 6 to October 28
Wednesdays, 3:30 p.m. - 6:00 p.m.

Contact: Kas Gurtler
PO Box 1384
Port Townsend, WA 98368
360-379-6957, ext. 119
www.ptguide.com/farmersmarket

PROSSER

PROSSER FARMERS MARKET

Location: Prosser City Park (7th & Sommers)
June to October
Saturdays, 8:00 a.m. - Noon

Contact: Linda Hall
1230 Bennett Avenue
Prosser, WA 99350
509-786-3600
www.quicktel.com/users/farmers

PUYALLUP

PUYALLUP FARMERS MARKET

Location: Pioneer Park (Meridian & Pioneer)
May 6 to September 2
Saturdays, 9:00 a.m. - 2:00 p.m.

Contact: Lynn Wallace
PO Box 1298
Puyallup, WA 98371
253-845-6755
www.puyallupchamber.com

RAYMOND

PUBLIC MARKET ON THE WILLAPA

Location: 4th & Heath
June 2 to September 30
Fridays & Saturdays, 10:00 a.m. -
5:00 p.m.

Contact: Carol Dunsmoor
PO Box 325
Raymond, WA 98577
360-942-4700
cdunsmoor@willapabay.org

SEATTLE

COLUMBIA CITY FARMERS MARKET

Location: 4801 Rainier Avenue S. & Edmunds
Street
May 31 to October 18
Wednesdays, 3:00 p.m. - 7:00 p.m.

Contact: Karen Kinney
4529 - 33rd Avenue S.
Seattle, WA 98118
206-722-4835
www.ci.seattle.wa.us/don/columbia

FREMONT FARMERS MARKET

Location: N. 34th & Fremont Avenue
May to October
Sundays, 10:00 a.m. - 4:00 p.m.

Contact: Judy Kirkhuff
6722 - 7th Avenue N.W.
Seattle, WA 98117
206-782-2286

PIKE PLACE PUBLIC MARKET

Location: First Avenue & Pike Street
Primary Farm Season
Mondays to Saturdays, 9:00 a.m. -
6:00 p.m., Sundays, 10:00 a.m. -
5:00 pm
Organic Farmer Days
June 18 to November 1
Wednesdays & Sundays, 10:00 a.m. -
4:00 p.m.

Contact: Mark Musick
85 Pike Street, Room 500
Seattle, WA 98101
206-682-7453, ext. 233
www.pikeplacemarket.org

UNIVERSITY DISTRICT
FARMERS MARKET

Location: NE 50th Street & University Way N.E.
May 27 to November 4
Saturdays, 9:00 a.m. - 2:00 p.m.

Contact: Chris Curtis
4519½ University Way N.E. #203
Seattle, WA 98105
206-547-2278
www.scn.org/earth/ufm/

WEST SEATTLE FARMERS MARKET

Location: California Avenue S.W.
& S.W. Alaska
June 18 to October 29
Sundays, 10:00 a.m. - 2:00 p.m.

Contact: Chris Curtis
4519½ University Way N.E. #203
Seattle, WA 98105
206-547-2278
www.scn.org/earth/ufm/

SELAH

SELAH FARMERS MARKET

Location: W. Naches Avenue & First Street
June 17 to November 4
Saturdays, 9:00 a.m. - 1:30 p.m.

Contact: Julie Morris
PO Box 415
Selah, WA 98942
509-697-5545

SEQUIM

SEQUIM OPEN AIRE MARKET

Location: Second & Cedar
May to October
Saturdays, 9:00 a.m. - 2:00 p.m.

Contact: Su Howat
PO Box 1817
Sequim, WA 98382
360-683-9446

SHELTON

SHELTON FARMERS MARKET

Location: Second & Railroad
May 6 to October 14
Saturdays, 10:00 a.m. - 3:00 p.m.

Contact: Deborah Parman
PO Box 1986
Shelton, WA 98584
360-427-4555

SNOHOMISH

SNOHOMISH FARMERS MARKET

Location: First Street (two blocks west of
Avenue D Bridge)
May 11 to September 28
Thursdays, 5:00 p.m. - Sunset

Contact: Marie Brayman
PO Box 1994
Snohomish, WA 98291
425-347-2790

SPOKANE

SPOKANE FARMERS' MARKET

Location: Division & Second Avenue
May 20 to October 28
Saturdays & Wednesdays, 8:00 a.m. -
1:00 p.m.

Contact: Brent Olsen
PO Box 7424
Spokane, WA 99207
509-685-1548
www.spokanefarmersmarket.
homestead.com

STANWOOD

STANWOOD VILLAGE FARMERS FAIRE

Location: Faire Stanwood Cinema Pavilion
(four miles west of I-5, Exit 212)
April to September
Saturdays & Sundays, 11:00 a.m. -
5:00 p.m.
October to December 17
Sundays, 11:00 a.m. - 5:00 p.m.

Contact: Joy Song Morgan-Nelson
PO Box 237
Silvana, WA 98287
360-652-0358
www.earthlink.net/~farmersmarket

TACOMA

PROCTOR FARMERS MARKET

Location: Insurance Parking Lot (4001 N. 26th
at Madison)
June 5 to September 18
Saturdays, 9:00 a.m. - 2:00 p.m.

Contact: Leah Walker
Bill Garl
3722 N. 31st Street
Tacoma, WA 98407
253-756-8901

TACOMA FARMERS MARKET

Location: Broadway, between 9th & 11th
June 1 to October 19
Thursdays, 9:00 a.m. - 2:00 p.m.

Contact: Stacy Ricker
PO Box 707
Tacoma, WA 98401
253-272-7077

TONASKET

TONASKET FARMERS MARKET

Location: Triangle Park (Western Avenue &
Hwy. 97)
June to October
Thursdays, 3:00 p.m. - 6:00 p.m.

Contact: Whispering Pine
PO Box 332
Tonasket, WA 98855
509-486-1395

UNIVERSITY PLACE

UNIVERSITY PLACE FARMERS MARKET

Location: Bridgeport Way W. & 36th at Clock
Tower (lower level)
May 6 to October 28
Saturdays, 10:00 a.m. - 3:00 p.m.

Contact: Terry Reim
Dixie Harris
3617 Bridgeport Way W.
University Place, WA 98466
253-564-6373
www.upfarmersmarket.com

VANCOUVER

VANCOUVER FARMERS MARKET

Location: Downtown Vancouver on Ester Street
between 8th & 6th (next to Ester
Short Park)
April 1 to October 28
Saturdays, 9:00 a.m. - 3:00 p.m.

Contact: Ann Amies
PO Box 61638
Vancouver, WA 98666
360-737-8298
www.vancouverfarmersmarket.com

VASHON

VASHON FARMERS MARKET

Location: Half block north of Bank Road on
Vashon Hwy. S.W.
April 1 to October 14
Saturdays, 9:00 a.m. - 2:00 p.m.

Contact: Richard Odell
PO Box 2894
Vashon, WA 98070
206-567-5293

WAPATO

WAPATO FARMERS MARKET

Location: Wapato Community Center,
1009 S. Camas Avenue (¼ mile
south of SR 97)
July 22 to September 9
Saturdays, 9:00 a.m. - 2:00 p.m.

Contact: Nancy Story
PO Box 67
Wapato, WA 98951
509-877-7553

WENATCHEE

WENATCHEE VALLEY FARMERS MARKET

Location: Riverfront Park (base of 5th Street)
June to October, & May 13, 20, 27
Wednesdays & Saturdays, 8:00 a.m. -
Noon

Location: Centennial Park (Wenatchee Avenue
& Kittitas Street)
June to August
Thursdays, 4:00 p.m. - 8:00 p.m.

Contact: Valerie Schooler
PO Box 2824
Wenatchee, WA 98807
509-667-1343

WEST RICHLAND

WEST RICHLAND FARMERS MARKET

Location: Flat Top Park (Bombing Range Road
& Van Giesen)
May 13 to October 28
Saturdays, 9:00 a.m. - 1:00 p.m.

Contact: Gail Clark
3801 W. Van Giesen
Richland, WA 99353
509-967-3431
www.westrichland.org

WOODINVILLE

WOODINVILLE FARMERS' MARKET

Location: City Hall - Soreson School at 175th
April 1 to October 14
Saturdays, 9:00 a.m. - 4:00 p.m.

Contact: Grant Davidson
PO Box 1927
Woodinville, WA 98072
425-485-1042

YAKIMA

YAKIMA FARMERS' MARKET

Location: S. 3rd Street at Yakima Avenue in
front of Capitol Theatre
June 4 to October 29
Sundays, 9:30 a.m. - 2:30 p.m.

Contact: Gina Smoot
PO Box 1076
Yakima, WA 98907
509-457-5765
www.yakimafarmersmarket.org

THIS LIST WAS PROVIDED TO YOU BY:

WASHINGTON STATE FARMERS MARKET ASSOCIATION (WSFMA)

PO Box 30727 • Seattle, WA 98103-0727
206-706-5198 • www.wafarmersmarkets.com
Zachary Lyons, WSFMA Director

WSFMA is a network of Farmers Markets across the state. It was created in 1978 as a nonprofit organization funded by member markets. It works with other agricultural groups and government agencies to provide workshops and marketing resources. They offer a brochure listing the current farmers markets operating in the state of Washington. If you're interested in becoming a market or associate member and receiving various benefits (which include a quarterly newsletter, annual conference, and more), contact their website or write for more information.

NATIONAL FARMERS MARKET DIRECTORY
USDA/AMS/TMD/WMDB
Room 2642–South
Independence Avenue, S.W.
Washington, DC 20250-0267

For more information, call 1-800-384-8704 or visit their website at www.ams.usda.gov

Organized by state, this directory lists known farmers markets operating in the United States. It is available at no charge.

Please see our website for the latest market directory updates, news, membership opportunities, and more.

Bibliography

BOOKS

Nava Atlas
Vegetariana
The Dial Press, 1984.

Better Homes & Gardens
Heritage Cook Book
Meredith Corporation, 1975.

Deni Bown
Encyclopedia of Herbs & Their Uses
Dorling Kindersley, 1995.

Ball, TMs Ball Corporation
BALL BLUE BOOK, Guide To Home Canning, Freezing & Dehydration
Alltrista Corporation, 1995.

Bremness, Lesley
The Complete Book of Herbs
Viking Penguin, 1988.

Castleman, Michael
The Healing Herbs
Rodale Press, 1991.

Liebster, Gunther
MACMILLAN BOOK OF Berry Gardening
Macmillan Publishing Co., 1986.

Melzer, Werner
BeeKeeping
Barron's Educational Series, Inc., 1989.

Morse, Roger A.
The ABC & XYZ of Bee Culture, 40th Edition
The A.I. Root Co., 1990.

National Gardening Association
Gardening: The Complete Guide to Growing America's Favorite Fruits & Vegetables
Addison-Wesley Publishing Co., 1986.

Nugent, Nancy
The Prevention Total Health System: Food and Nutrition
Rodale Press, Inc., 1983

Reader's Digest
Eat Better, Live Better
The Reader's Digest Association, Inc., 1982.

Riotte, Louise
Sleeping With A Sunflower
Garden Way Publishing, 1987.

Rupp, Rebecca
Blue Corn and Square Tomatoes
Garden Way Publishing, 1987.

Spitzer, Theodore Morrow, and Hilary Baum
Public Markets and Community Revitalization
ULI—Urban Land Institute and Project for Public Spaces, Inc., 1995.

Taylor, Ronald J.
Northwest Weeds
Mountain Press Publishing Co., 1990.

CATALOGS

Goodwin Creek Gardens
PO Box 83
Williams, Oregon 97544
541-846-7357.

Integrated Fertility Management (IFM)
333 Ohme Gardens Road
Wenatchee, Washington 98801
509-662-3179.

Nichols Garden Nursery
1190 North Pacific Highway
Albany, Oregon 97321-4580
541-928-9280.

One Green World.
28696 S. Cramer Road
Molalla, Oregon 97038-8576
503-651-3005

Pinetree Garden Seeds
Box 300
New Gloucester, Maine 04260
207-926-3400

Raintree Nursery
391 Butts Road
Morton, Washington 98365
360-496-6400

Territorial Seed Company
PO Box 157
Cottage Grove, Oregon 97424
541-942-9547.

Totally Tomatoes
PO Box 1626
Augusta, Georgia 30903
803-663-0016

Index

Sidebar information is italicized.

C

Sidebar information is italicized.

Sidebar information is italicized.

Sidebar information is italicized.

Sidebar information is italicized.

Sidebar information is italicized.

Sidebar information is italicized.